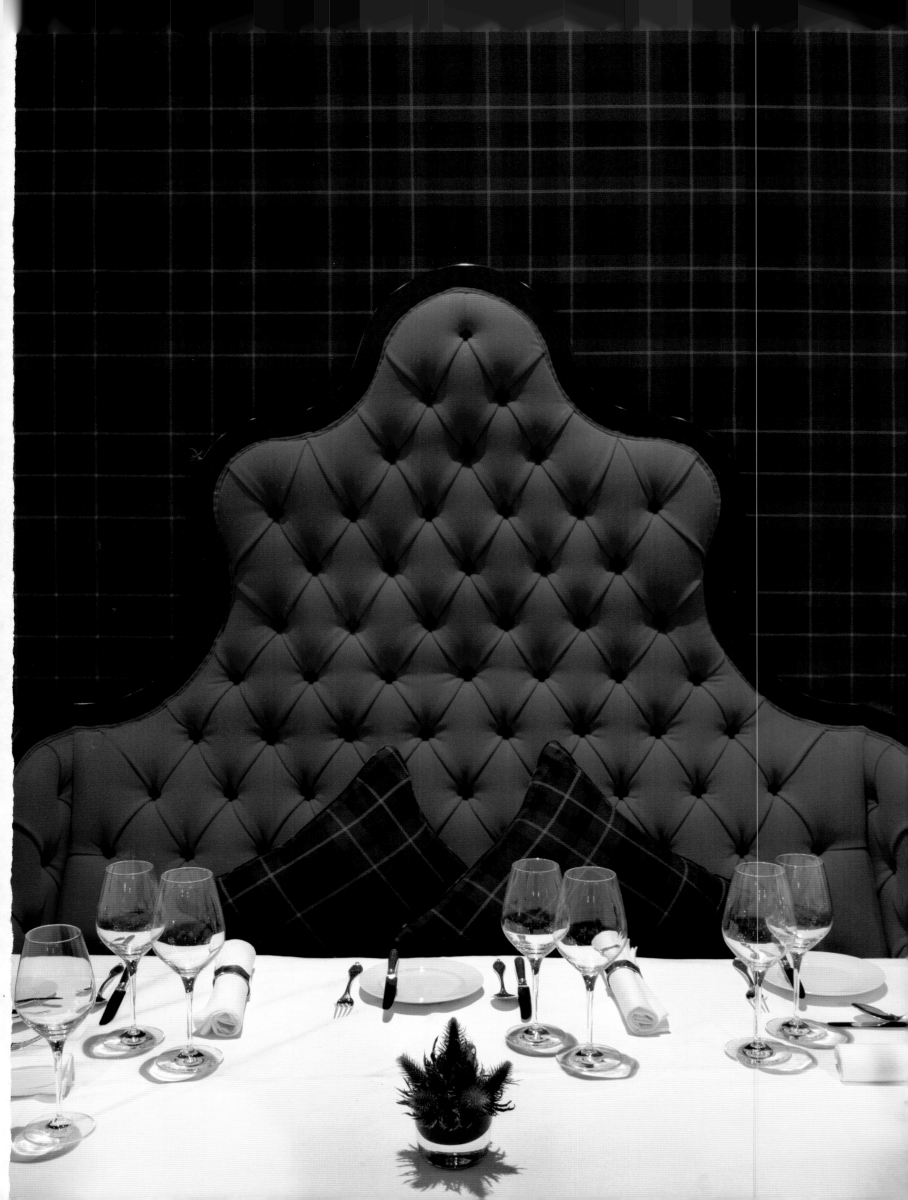

TARTANA, OR THE PLAID

I sing the plaid, and sing with all my skill,
Mount then, O fancy, standard to my will;
Be strong each thought, run soft each happy line,
That gracefulness and harmony may shine,
Adapted to the beautiful design.
Great is the subject, vast th'exalted theme,
And shall stand fair in endless rolls of fame.

An excerpt from the poem by Allan Ramsay, 1780

For Elise,
Plaidfully Yours!
Jeffrey Banks

TARTAN
Romancing the Plaid

JEFFREY BANKS AND DORIA DE LA CHAPELLE
FOREWORD BY ROSE MARIE BRAVO

RIZZOLI
NEW YORK

CONTENTS

Opposite: A tartan skirt in a photo by Gianni
Penati. *Vogue* 1967/Condé Nast Archives/Corbis.

FOREWORD

Rose Marie Bravo

In 1997 when I accepted the role of chief executive at Burberry, little did I know as I moved my family to England, that my story and my life would be in inextricably linked with the story of tartan and the Burberry plaid, or what is lovingly called in the United Kingdom "the check."

The small team that we had selected began to delve into the archives of this very British 150-year-old company. It became exceedingly clear that the Burberry trench coat with its plaid lining was the company's primary icon which conferred instantly on the wearer a sense of quality, status, class, and taste.

As I traveled around the world in an effort to understand the DNA and the magic of the brand, I was fascinated by the universal appeal and the emotion that all things tartan had in various cultures. Tartan is an unspoken language that can ellicit a response without one word being spoken. It has the ability to cross national borders, appeal to all generations and both genders. I studied an elderly Italian gentleman in a small village in the middle of Italy proudly sporting his tartan cap or Burberry scarf with a loden coat as well as a twenty-five-year-old gal on the streets of Seoul wearing the same items, creating a totally different impression in my mind.

Tartan and plaid, as this book will demonstrate, have the ability to send a variety of messages. I recalled my days merchandising department stores where from time to time several fashion designers would use tartan and plaid in a variety of ways. The most avant-garde creative people used it with a sense of irreverence. How could something so old be made to look modern and hip? A few designers would use plaid in its most traditional manner and color combinations and thus ellicit a sense of heritage, classicism, and longevity in the clothes. Even the manner in which tartan can take color in those unique exciting combinations can add so much personality and style to an ensemble.

In the United Kingdom tartan and plaid are ubiquitous. In your daily life you see these patterns used in so many venues and ways they enter your subconscious. So many fine establishments—hotels, restaurants, even castles—use tartan in their décor, and one has an immediate sense of home and belonging, warmth, coziness. You are just waiting for that delicious sweet-smelling, very hot tea to be poured into a fine china cup and saucer.

Walking the streets of London on a brisk, gray autumn day one of the most joyous sights would be to see a flock of young children out for a stroll wearing their subtle tartan jumpers or trousers. So, as you browse or read through this beautiful book, enjoy all the dimensions and the references that these patterns can ellicit. Yes, think England and its heritage and the royals, and Scotland and its clans and their pride. And see plaid as a fiery, irreverent banner in fashion and during the holidays where a tartan bow tie speaks volumes about its wearer. But most of all become seduced by the power, the magic, and the mystery inherent in this oldest and most exuberant expression of belonging.

Opposite: Burberry's Rose Marie Bravo presenting prizes of a Burberry raincoat and bag to Prince Charles following a charity fundraiser at Cirencester Polo Club, England.

INTRODUCTION

"It is not generally appreciated how vague is the knowledge of the tartans to which so many people pay homage. Where so little is known, so much is felt . . ."[1]

—Donald C. Stewart

Whenever the word tartan is mentioned, scores of exuberant images unfurl. Like a flag, tartan evokes the Scottish nation and its colorful kilted clans. It resonates with the wail of bagpipes. It snaps to attention with its smart, symmetrical design. But tartan is more than a design, it is a sign; and while it signifies kinship (real or imagined), country, and celebration to the Scots, its subtext is dignity, distinctiveness, and a sense of belonging—qualities that possess universal appeal. That is perhaps one reason why tartan, a textile indigenous to the Highlands, has evolved into one of the world's most popular fabrics, beloved by just about everyone, Scot or not.

In this book, we trace tartan's checkered history from the folkloric to the popular to the politically rebellious; from the regimental to the royal and fashionable; from the establishment to the antiestablishment, and finally to the

Opposite: A painting of Sir James MacDonald and his brother Sir Alexander MacDonald, attributed to William Mosman (circa 1750). This study of the MacDonald siblings indicates the lack of importance of tartan as a badge of clanship during this period, as four different setts can be distinguished on the garments that are depicted.
Right: Princely charm: Charles at Balmoral, 1978.

marketable and modern. As its history unfolds, you will discover tartan's ability to transcend the clans that claim it, allowing us all to endow it with our own meanings. Along the way, we'll examine tartan plaid in all its glorious warp and weft to determine how and why this humble fabric, so indelibly linked with ancestry, ceremony, history, and tradition has become "a supreme option of style and meaning and use in our time."[2]

In several ways this book departs from standard tartan tomes. It approaches the subject with both a respect for history and a healthy skepticism for mist-laden lore. Neither a registry of the hundreds of author-ized tartans in the world, nor a scholarly study, *Tartan* attempts to kick up the pleated kilt, revealing through a combination of fact, anecdote, psychological insight, and a tad of irreverence, the underlying reasons why the madness for plaid not only endures but flourishes.

TRADITION: TARTAN'S EARLY BEGINNINGS

The "Tradition" chapter of the book sheds light on the folkloric origins of the plaid in the Highlands, the rugged northern part of Scotland that was separated geographically, culturally, religiously, and linguistically from the Lowlands—and as a result developed its own distinctive form of dress. We highlight the essence of tartan, analyzing its weaving techniques, and explaining how the yarns were dyed. While tartan was part of early Highland culture, it did not exist in a form we would recognize today: the checked fabric was woven in natural and vegetable-dyed wool, with red being the preferred shade. Prior to the sixteenth century, Highland dress for men was a shirt and, over it, a plaid known as the "big wrap" (or in Gaelic the *Feiladh Mor*), a very basic garment made of a length of

Left: Nifty '50s tartan—a dolman-sleeved coat from Harrods, London, 1955.

THE CRITICS' PRIZE MUSICAL

BRIGADOON

Book and Lyrics by
ALAN JAY LERNER

Music by
FREDERICK LOEWE

"SMASH MUSICAL HIT!"
— WALTER WINCHELL

Opposite: Highland hijinks—dancers perform at the
Braemar Highland Games, 1953.
Right: A poster for the smash hit Lerner and Loewe musical
Brigadoon, caricaturing Scottish Highland dancers, 1954.

fabric that was first pleated, then wrapped around the body and belted, with a skirtlike lower half, and an upper portion that swathed over the shoulder. Dressed in such a way, the men of the Highlands were often referred to as "red shanks" (or bare-legged) and prided themselves on their ability to withstand the rigors of their wet, harsh climate.

By mid-sixteenth century, there is more written evidence of tartan on record, although since the word tartan meant not only a checked fabric, but also a type of cloth, the meaning is not always clear. However, according to Hugh Cheape, principal curator of the National Museums of Scotland, "it is not until the late seventeenth or even early eighteenth century that any uniformity was adopted by family, clan, or district. The evolution of the plaid was the key factor in Highland dress. It was simple to make, versatile, and classless— it was worn by the lowest and highest."[3]

The seventeenth century was a pivotal period for tartan: In Highland society the Gaelic bards had always sung the praises of the clan, but with the rise in political and religious upheavals, they came to regard tartan

as a potent symbol in itself, and the word began to be used to denote nobility, dignity, and a sense of style and taste. We note how the Celtic notion of "personal display" gathered momentum, particularly when the clans went to war—which they did with frequency. The Catholic, Gaelic-speaking Highlanders skirmished with their neighbors, the politically powerful, English-speaking Presbyterians. When opponents of James II, the Catholic Stuart king, dethroned him in 1688 so that his daughter Mary and her Dutch Protestant husband William of Orange could ascend to power, the followers of James II staged a rebellion. Bloody battles ensued, pitting Jacobites (those loyal to James II who took their names from Jacobus, Latin for "James") against the government, and tartan became a deeply important symbol of the Jacobite cause.

Tartan's symbolic value reached a critical mass in 1707, when the British parliament passed the Act of Union, disbanding the separate Scottish parliament in exchange for a number of economic benefits. In their anger at the act, Lowlanders joined their Highland neighbors in using tartan as a means of registering

Opposite: Patchworked plaid—tartan patches applied to distressed denim jeans create great graphics, from Abercrombie & Fitch, 2003.

Below: Light infantry, circa 1853—an officer of the 74th Highlanders, a division that was granted permission to wear tartan trousers instead of kilts.

Below: The answer to everyone's question as to what is worn under a kilt— Black Watch soldier in Hong Kong on a windy day.
Opposite: Spy drawing of Jeffrey Mackie on a Highland stroll.

Below: Portrait of John Campbell, Lord Glenorchy, later 3rd Earl of Breadalbane painted by Enoch Seeman in the 1720s.

Opposite: Rocker Rod Stewart with his horse, Mia. Stewart, who was born in London, has a long association with Scotland and is particularly passionate about its football side.

their protest. For the first time, tartan, seen on some of Edinburgh's most influential ladies, became the "national color." By the time Prince Charles Edward Stewart ("Bonnie Prince Charlie") chose tartan Highland dress as the uniform for himself and his army in the ultimate Jacobite War of 1745, the symbolic worth of tartan seemed forever sealed.

The crushing defeat of the Jacobites in the Battle of '45 had disastrous repercussions, including the Proscription Act, which banned for thirty-seven years not only arms but also any form of Highland dress (except in the military). Ironically, instead of making tartan disappear, the act ultimately served to galvanize clan-consciousness. Reports of the bravery and success demonstrated by the Highland regiments in various wars, both in Europe and America, also helped raise the status of tartan to an all-time high.

With a growing appreciation for European Romanticism, writers such as historical novelist Walter Scott, whose work glorified the Highlander and his existence, added even more panache to the plaid. At the same time, Highland societies were organized to trace clan tartans and codify them, preserving their lineage for generations to come.

Central to the success of the tartan revival is George IV,

who in 1822 became the first English king in almost 150 years to visit Edinburgh. Something of a costume buff, George was persuaded to appear in full tartan regalia, thereby assuring that his Scottish audience would do the same. The "plaided panorama" and the tartan mania that ensued provided an excellent living for tartan manufacturers and created a major industry that continues to thrive. As Hugh Cheape notes, "'Highland dress' [had been] turned into 'tartan costume.' A practical dress with style became in the nineteenth century a fashionable dress with little regard for function."[4]

Royal influence on tartan grew and prospered during the reign of Queen Victoria and her consort Prince Albert, who, by establishing a permanent residence at Balmoral Castle in the Highlands, really put Scotland and tartan on the map. The Highlands became a tourist destination and tartan became the object of frenzied interest. The Sobieski-Stuarts, two brothers with artistic and social aspirations, claiming to be the heirs of Bonnie Prince Charlie, published a richly illustrated book, cataloguing the details of known and unknown Scottish clan tartans, thereby inciting a rush to lay claim to the tartan to which one's family was "entitled." Suddenly tartan was in vogue.

FASHION

Tartan dress has always had an element of style to it, but not until the nineteenth century, as a result of the Napoleonic Wars, did it develop a patina of European sophistication. Fashion catalogues from the Victorian and Edwardian eras featured fabulous tartan creations from *couturiers* in Paris, often in silk, that were fitted, poufed, and flounced. Given the new aniline dyes that yielded brighter colors, tartan dressing became more striking than ever. Whereas up until this time, tartan has been reserved principally for menswear, it now became an important fabric for women's clothing.

The unique wardrobe of Edward VIII, the Duke of Windsor, set a standard for men's dress that has never been equaled. The duke may have abdicated the Crown, but he never considered giving up tartan. From young boyhood, through his dotage, the duke adored tartan and put it together with great originality, piling pattern on pattern. His wife, Wallis, Duchess of Windsor, also appeared in tartan, but her plaid dresses were whipped up by couturier Christian Dior.

Tartan had become synonymous with the style of the British upper classes, who had long been wearing it not only for its stylishness, but also for its ability to

Below: The plaided princesses—England's Princesses Elizabeth and sister Margaret Rose offering a biscuit to their Corgi at Balmoral.
Following pages: The royal treatment—H.M. Queen Elizabeth II in 1972 dancing at the Ghillies' Ball on her Balmoral estate in Scotland, and a debutante-draped tartan on the cover of *Harper's Bazaar*, 1950.

withstand the rigors of stable and paddock and walks on the misty moors. It wasn't long before that aristocratic association endowed tartan with an aspirational air of exclusivity, gentility, and belonging with which people everywhere were only too happy to cloak themselves.

While tartan continued to be worn as a perennial sportive favorite throughout the majority of the twentieth century, in the late 1970s, it spread in a different direction, bearing out the maxim that "fashion will adopt the uniforms of rebellion." For disenfranchised youth throughout Great Britain, punk music channeled their discontent and disillusionment with government and modern society, and tartan was worn ironically as an antiestablishment symbol. Designers like Vivienne Westwood explained that they had "seized the very fabric of the establishment in order to reverse its meaning." In acts that symbolized punk's spirit of rebellion and transgression, tartan was ripped and torn and safety-pinned with creative audacity.

But tartan has always been paradoxical, embodying "yin and yang": While it symbolizes the fierce independence and heroism of the Highland warrior, at the same time it conjures the uniformity of the Black Watch military regiments, marching in step with perfect precision. Whereas some favor tartan in its rebellious

HARPER'S

Bazaar

Scottish Number

August 1950

Previous pages: Skirt-chasing—a rush of tartan pleats. Photo by Arthur Elgort/*Vogue* 1991. © Condé Nast Publications.

Opposite: Vivienne Westwood's jabot-frothed tartan dandy.

Below: Wedded to tartan—Kate Moss as Vivienne Westwood's bride in the finale of her "Anglomania" autumn/winter 1993–94 show.

mode, others share a vision that hews closer to the traditional. Certainly Ralph Lauren, self-confessed Anglophile, has employed tartan in an extraordinary range. His women's fall/winter collections almost invariably include some wonderful new take on tartan—whether patterned in sequins on a cashmere halter-necked top or swept into a gorgeous taffeta ball gown. Lauren also champions the plaid for men, and his distinctive menswear invariably features both elegantly cut gentlemen's tartan clothing and beefed-up country plaids.

As different as their approaches to tartan might be, designers Westwood and Lauren often turn to the same illustrious tartan weaver, Lochcarron of Scotland. The firm's owner, descendant of a long line of weavers who were once commissioned to weave a special tweed for George V, produces the largest range of authentic tartans, covering the spectrum from pipe bands to the latest couture creation for Alexander McQueen.

The resurgence of Burberry is one of the most dramatic stories in the history of tartan. Best known for its gabardine trench coats, lined with the distinctive Burberry

tartan, the firm turned the lining inside out in a moment of public relations genius, and started marketing the tartan itself as a symbol of the firm and its inherent traditional British quality. Today, the iconic tartan is synonymous with luxury and classic style. Burberry's super status is in part owed to designer Christopher Bailey, who was hired by CEO Rose Marie Bravo in 2001 to design the company's Prorsum line. Blending Burberry's longstanding reputation and name recognition with hip street chic, Bailey parlayed the pattern into serious, acclaimed couture. He is credited with catapulting the tartan and the firm to global prominence. Currently, it would almost be impossible to walk the streets of a major city in the civilized world without spotting the distinctive check.

The number of notable American and European designers who are passionate about plaid give proof of its enduring thrall. Among others whom tartan has inspired and whose designs are highlighted here are: Jean-Paul Gaultier, Alexander McQueen, Paul Smith, Marc Jacobs for Louis Vuitton, Christian Lacroix, Isaac Mizrahi, Yves St. Laurent, and Michael Kaye.

LIVING

As tartan became more fashionable, its parameters increased. If you could drape a woman's body with tartan, why not drape a wall? Queen Victoria and Prince Albert were arguably the original tartan interior designers, decking the halls, walls, and windows of Balmoral with their favorite tartans, and even dolling up their carriage windows with the plaid. Tartan's rich colors and comforting grids are a dream to decorate with, and because most patterns include multiple colors, plaid frequently works to unify all the other fabrics in a room. In the case of Glen Feshie, a Scottish baronial castle whose estate borders Balmoral, designers Ward Denton and Christopher Gardner use subtle, ancient tartans to bring warmth and intimacy to the grandly proportioned rooms. In a decidedly different way, Bill Diamond and Tony Baratta decorate with a profusion of plaids, often in bright colors and over-the-top proportions, lending a Pop-art quality to their rooms. And ANTA, a Scottish textile and ceramic maker, brings an original and

Right: Making a grand entrance—a slim tartan evening coat over a white bias-cut column. Henry Clark/ *Vogue* 1958/Condé Nast Archives/Corbis.

Following left page: Scotch neat—trim tartan waistcoat, bonnet, gloves, and brolly à la 1950s

Following right page: Two 1950s models in the slim silhouette of the era—dressmaker blouses, tartan pencil skirts, and, of course, gloves. Sante Forlano/Condé Nast Archives/Corbis.

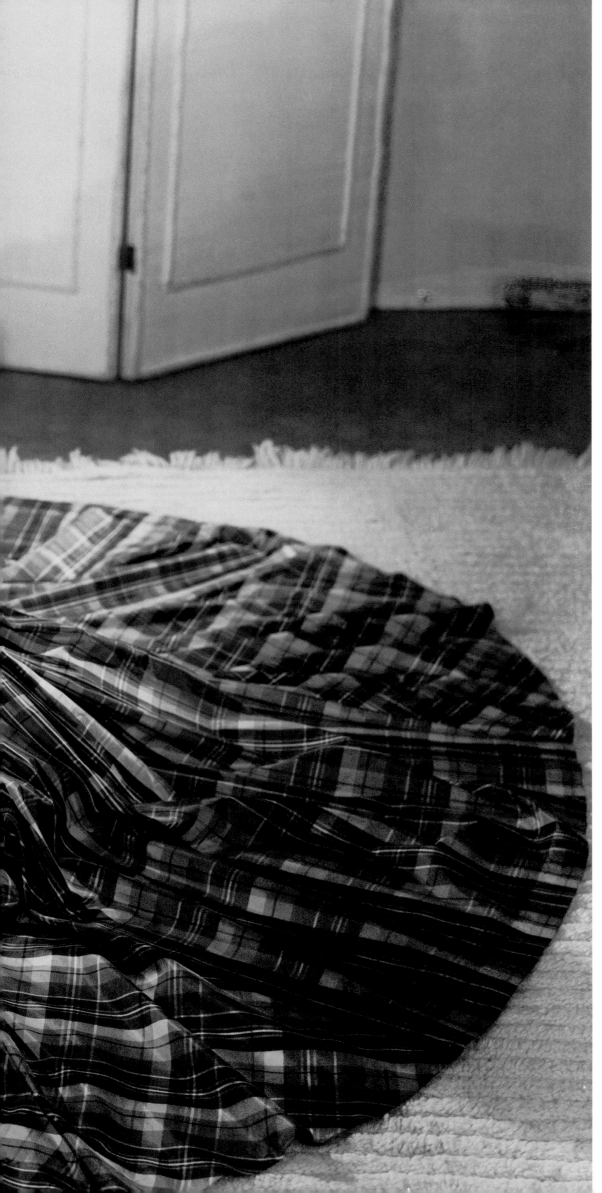

Previous left page: All about Ava—A young Ava Gardner rehearsing her lines in a tartan topper, circa 1950.

Previous right page: Silent screen star Gloria Swanson, in an "ensemble" designed by Rene Hubert of Fox Studios for the film *Music in the Air*. She is wearing a black velvet coat with tartan collar over a black-and-white tartan gown with marching tartan gloves and ruffled tartan muff!

Left: We Love Lucy—actress/comedienne Lucille Ball surrounded by a sea of tartan taffeta skirted dress with fitted black top, circa 1942.

Opposite: Muscular tartan— macho kilt and cap from Abercrombie & Fitch, 2003.
Below: A detail of the salon at Glen Feshie Lodge in Scotland.

organic approach to tartan, weaving colors that reflect the Scottish landscape into their spare and simple designs.

But the chapter "Living" is not only about living in beautifully decorated rooms: it is also about how tartan transforms other spaces we inhabit, including the worlds of window display, store design, ballet, theater, and film. We begin a tartan tour of Tiffany's magical holiday windows, filled with miniature Christmas baubles, and Randall A. Ridless's Burberry interiors, influenced by the firm's iconic check. We'll glance at Madonna's "Re-Invention" tour, Gwen Stefani's tartan fling, and madly plaided Tartan Week shows like the spectacular "Dressed to Kilt," featuring everyone from Sean Connery to New York City's bravest firemen sauntering down the catwalk in kilts. And we check out *Braveheart, Brigadoon, Rob Roy, Union Jack*, and *Sex and the City*, finding that tartan is as theatrical and festive as it is comforting.

And to conclude the book, we leave you with the fruits of our extensive research to provide the reader with what we believe are the "tops in tartan"—the world's best resources for authentic tartan goods, gear, and accessories.

If tartan embodies beauty, theater, harmony, exclusivity, and style, is it any wonder that even those of us who are not Macdonalds, Campbells, or Grants by birth, have

Opposite: Tartan terry toweling from Ralph Lauren and
Brooks Brothers pajamas. Arthur Elgort/*Vogue*,
September 1991/© Condé Nast Publications.
Below: Ralph Lauren's Black Watch–patterned saddle.

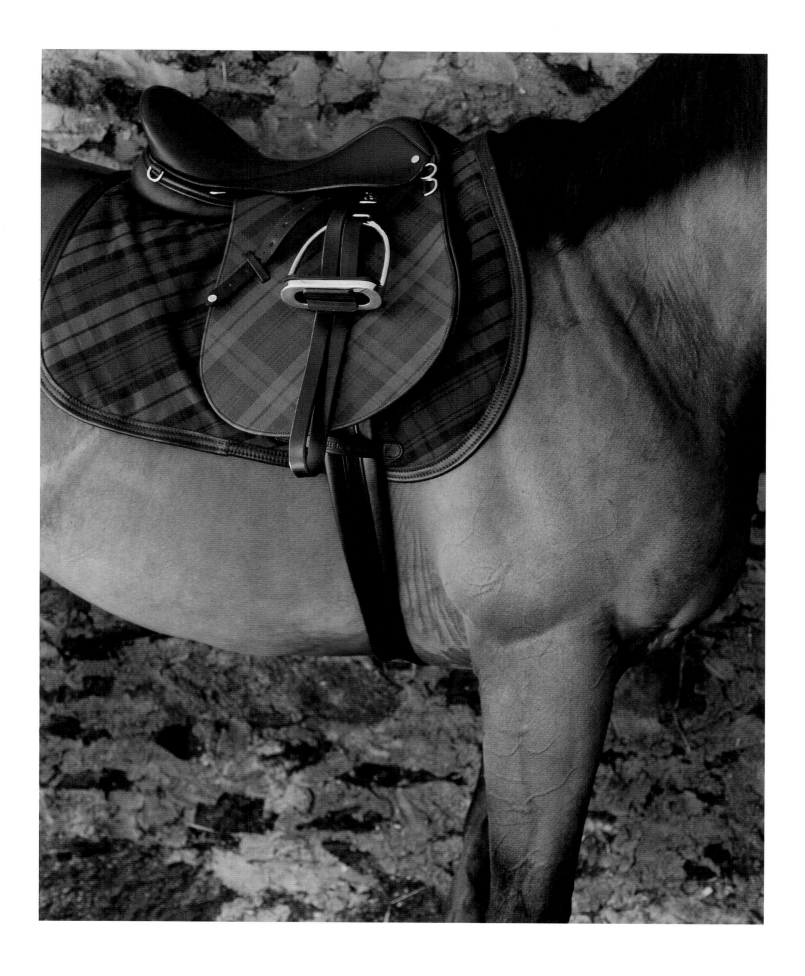

Opposite: Vivienne Westwood in her own tartan bondage suit, 1977. Tim Jenkins/*WWD/* © Condé Nast Publications.

Below: Singer Gwen Stefani, a tartan aficionado, and the Harajuku girls at the 2004 Billboard Music Awards in Las Vegas.

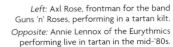

Left: Axl Rose, frontman for the band Guns 'n' Roses, performing in a tartan kilt.
Opposite: Annie Lennox of the Eurythmics performing live in tartan in the mid-'80s.

co-opted the meaning of tartan, tailoring it to our needs? Consider, for example, our penchant for checked school uniforms or preppy plaids: We respond not only to their cheery colors, but also to their orderly patterns that subliminally suggest structure, pedigree, and social position, endowing us with instant insider status. Part of tartan's magnetism and its longevity is its ability to integrate a community beneath its patterns, to convey a sense of belonging.

Tartan's allure is both democratic and noble, establishment and antiestablishment, high and low: It was worn by clansmen and clan chieftain, and men, women, and children alike. The plaid is also highly organized: its carefully ruled lines and grids provide logic, parameters, and boundaries. As a result, architects and artists, designers of fashion and interiors draw inspiration from it, and people who wear it seem to find reassurance in its repeated rectilinear lines.

According to psychologist Michael Picucci:

Tartan appeals to our "old brain," the primitive part of us that is instinct-driven and draws upon nature to inform our choices. As we use fashion and clothing to experiment with our identities, empathic associations are created. Sometimes those associations yearn for the grounding of our ancestors (real or archetypal). We draw upon their energies for both comfort and the ongoing need for self-reclamation and self-expression …This yearning is the language of the soul.[5]

Never was this yearning more apparent than in the aftermath of September 11, 2001, in New York City. Women who would never have been seen in anything but the latest designer du jour were photographed in all manner of tartan on Manhattan's Fifth Avenue by *New York Times* photographer Bill Cunningham. Tiffany's windows displayed warm fireside scenes with patchwork tartan stockings hung by the chimney and tiny woodland creatures sporting tartan top hats along with their Tiffany diamonds. Record numbers of brides swept down the aisle swathed in tartan. It would seem that just as the Scottish clansmen of old clung to their plaids as a badge of identity, so do we wrap ourselves in our tartans and seek refuge in an often less-than-orderly world.

Below left: To disenfranchised British youth, a mohawk was one way to show rebellion and tartan was another.

Below right: Malcolm McLaren, a leader in the British punk movement, manager of the band the Sex Pistols, as well as then-husband and business partner of Vivienne Westwood, displays his displeasure at the existing social structure with both T-shirt and tartan.

TRADITION

"Tartan is both structure and story. Its story is the very romance of history; its structure is the systematic ordering of the world in line and color."[1]

Tartan is most assuredly ancient but its origins are obscure, and its history, both literal and symbolic, is endlessly open to debate. Some claim that tartan is as old as the Highland clans it came to signify; others maintain the fabric did not acquire its status as a badge of kinship and belonging until the late eighteenth or early nineteenth century.

There is no debate, however, over tartan's universal popularity: Its riotous colors and repeated patterns both comfort and charm; its intrinsic pedigree reassures; and its aura of romance enthralls us all.

But what really is tartan? According to Hugh Cheape, principal curator at the National Museums of Scotland, "its definition can move from the physical to the metaphysical, from the utilitarian to the aesthetic: On the one

Opposite: General William Gordon of Fyvie, in the warrior-hero pose, painted in 1776 by Pompeo Girolamo Batoni. The officer's plaid references the draping of a Roman toga against a purely classical background.

Checks and stripes were certainly not unique to Scotland. The pattern is almost as primitive a weave as is possible to make, and evidence of checked fabric existed in other prehistoric cultures. E.J.W. Barber, noted primitive textile historian, tells in her book *Prehistoric Textiles: The Development of Cloth in the Neolithic and Bronze Age* of the Halstatt culture which flourished from 100 B.C.E. to 400 B.C.E. throughout much of Austria, Switzerland, eastern France, and beyond, and produced some brilliantly colored checked patterns that were unearthed in Salzburg's salt mines where they had been remarkably preserved. Although there were natural whites, beiges, and browns, many of the woolen yarns were dyed rich copper-reds, blues, and olive greens.

hand, tartan is simply a check or pattern in a variety of colours in woven fabric in which bands of colour are repeated in equal proportion in warp (running lengthwise) and weft (running across); and on the other, it is a national symbol for all Scotland and a cultural icon for Scotland and 'Scottishness' throughout the world."[2] Steeped in social, political, and religious Highland history, tartan is imbued with meaning and intellectual and emotional resonance, elevating it well beyond the realm of the merely plaid.

Even the word "tartan" is tinged with controversy and color. Histories of the plaid have traditionally maintained that the word "tartan" entered the Scottish language via the French term *tiretaine*, which described a half wool, half linen cloth of any color. That explanation seems logical, since the word was first used during the early sixteenth century when Scotland and France enjoyed an extended period of political and cultural association under what the Scots termed the Auld Alliance. More recently, though, the etymological link with the French has been carefully reconsidered, and it has been convincingly argued that the word "tartan"

may well derive, instead, from a Scottish Gaelic word denoting a textile design with patterns of crossing colors. The term can be identified with the cognate *tarsainn* in modern Scottish Gaelic.[3] This would situate the word's origin in the Highlands—the place with which it always has been most closely identified and where it has been worn most proudly.

The Highlands, of course, didn't have a patent on the plaid: The decorative weaving of stripes and checks (stripes crossing at right angles) is recognized as probably the earliest form of patterned fabric anywhere. In the National Museum of Scotland, a fragment of fabric dating from the third century C.E. and excavated from Falkirk, near the Roman-built Antonine Wall, shows a twill weave rendered in dark and light natural shades of wool. (The word "twill" is derived from the same root as "two"; twills are built on an "over two, under two" weaving pattern.) The third-century fragment, known as the Falkirk Tartan, is considered the earliest known example of the Highland plaid.

Although tartan can dazzle with its seeming complexity, its method of production is relatively simple.

Opposite: William Cumming, piper to the Laird of Grant in a portrait by Richard Waitt of 1714. He wears a form of livery comprised of red-and-yellow tartan and as part of the feudal chief's panoply, carries the banner and coat of arms of the Grant family.

> *"Tartan owes much of its beauty and liveliness to the interplay of color and the action of light and sight along and across the diagonal ribs of the twill weave that is traditionally used in making the cloth."* —James D. Scarlett, in his seminal work, *Tartan, The Highland Textile*

Different colored yarns are woven usually in a plain twill to produce a check of colors and blends. (Blends are created wherever two colors of thread cross to produce a third color; thus, two yarn shades produce a three-color combination.) The arrangement of colored threads is the same in the warp (running lengthwise) as in the weft (running across), giving the design balance and symmetry. This is how a tartan pattern is created:

> *In detail, colored yarns are counted into bands of different width when the weaver sets up the threads on the warp and this is described as the thread count. The same sequence of yarns in colors and widths is then woven in the weft to achieve a check of regular pattern. Each section of the design mirrors the section next to it. The thread counts of the different colored yarns act as a key to the patterns or setts.*[4]

Color—and how it is worked—is pivotal to tartan design. Each stripe of the warp crosses every stripe of the weft, so when vertical and horizontal stripes of the same color cross, the result is solid color at the point of intersection. When, however, a stripe crosses another of a different color, the result is a mixture of the two colors in equal proportions. Thus, tartans should be composed of clear, bright colors, but ones sufficiently soft to blend well and thereby create new shades. One of the paradoxical qualities of tartan, according to James D. Scarlett, is that "two colors, i.e., a simple check, give only one mixture (three shades in all) but six colors give fifteen mixtures, twenty-two shades: Thus, the more colors to begin with, the more subdued the final effect."[5]

Early Scottish weavers were dependent upon readily accessible dyes for many of their tartan colors. Some of the original dyes were acquired locally from natural sources, both plant and mineral. Owing to diverse soil conditions, there was a great deal of variation in available colors from district to district. Lichen that proliferated in the Highlands was used to create purples, yellows, and browns. Reds and other purples came from sources including dandelion root, bramble, Lady's Bedstraw, and St. John's wort. Other sources tell of additional color-yielding flora like birch leaves, sorrel, nettle, and of course, heather. But it is not valid to suggest that native dye plants alone were used in tartan production: The most difficult (and therefore most prized and expensive) colors to produce were vivid reds and blues. Scholars believe that these colors came to Scotland via trade up and down the west coast of Britain. A favorite blue, indigo, was imported in the early eighteenth century with such frequency that

In solchem Habit Gehen die 800 In Stettin angekom
oder Irren.

G. Köler Excud

Es ist ein Starckes dauerhafftigs Volck behilfft sich mit geringer speiß hatt es
Würtzeln, Wans auch die Notturfft erfordert Können sie des Tages Uber
meil weges lauffen, haben neben Musqueden Jhre Bogen vnd Köcher vnd

en Irrländer

ht brodt ſo Eſſen ſie
20 Teützſcher
 nge Meſſer.

Left: The earliest known image of Scottish soldiers in tartan—A German broadsheet made from a woodcut from 1631, depicting Highlanders (who were sometimes mistakenly described as "Irrelander oder Irren," i.e., Irish). It is assumed these men were part of MacKay's Regiment who served under Gustavus Adolphus in Stettin (now Szcezin, Poland). What is also interesting is the variety of dress illustrated: belted plaids, draped plaids, and one soldier in tartan breeches and tartan hose.

Opposite: A portrait of the young James Moray, son of the 13th Laird of Abercairney, was painted by Jeremiah Davison in the mid-eighteenth century. The lad was born in 1739 and died in 1768, predeceasing his father.

Right: A portrait of Kenneth, 3rd Lord Duffus by Richard Waite, whose family adopted the Sutherland name after an earldom was created in their favor in the former Viking Southland. He is dressed in a belted plaid of mostly red, black, and yellow tartan and tartan patterned hose, representing an aristocratic figure in Gaelic society. He is portrayed here as the image of the "deer hunter" in Gaelic praise poetry.

Andrew Fletcher, a member of parliament protesting the Act of Union of 1707 (which facilitated the trade of goods like indigo but involved dissolving the Scottish Parliament in favor of a united British parliament in Westminster) disparagingly declared, "the independence of our country was sold for some sugar, hogsheads, indigo, and stinking tobacco."[6]

The Highlanders were typically resourceful in their approach to the dyeing process. Whereas town dwellers would have dyed their woven cloth in a large vat, the Highlanders—who closely monitored the secrets of their trade—dyed their wool before it was spun, a process that required less space. Ever pragmatic, the weavers no doubt realized the timesaving device of using the same warp patterns over and over again. Economically minded, they saved the expensive dyes for fine-lined overchecks that, requiring very little pigment, produced a striking overlay color for modest investment of dye.[7]

Highland weavers also are thought to have shared the same basic pattern throughout a fairly large geographical area, with one weaver passing a pattern on to the next, who might then vary the design in minute ways to make it identifiable as a product of its district. We can probably infer that, for example, a given pattern that had become identified with the people of one clan and one locale thus became the prototype of that group's so-called "clan tartan."

It is important here to clarify what the word "clan" denotes. The word derives from the Gaelic term *clann*, which literally means "offspring" or "children," but is understood to signify family, kith, and kin. Technically, the word "clan" should apply only to the chief's family and those branches thereof who could furnish proof of descent from him; the word has, however, been extended to include all those who acknowledged the authority of a chief and accepted his protection.[8] Thus, in actuality, few members of a large clan are actually tied by blood to their chief. But the concept of clan loyalty was always stressed as it forged powerful ties that could be relied upon during battle.

The notion of a possible district or clan tartan is corroborated in Martin Martin's *A Description of the Western Islands of Scotland*, published in 1703, where he relates

A particularly vibrant red extracted from cochineal (the bodies of small, dried beetlelike insects imported from the Caribbean) began to be used in tartan dyes in the early seventeenth century. By the end of the eighteenth century, after the British government imposed the proscription prohibiting the wearing of any tartan at all in the Highlands, this cochineal-derived "scarlet" red assumed political significance when it became the color of protest for Scottish noblemen who commissioned portraits of themselves in Highland costume in an expression of defiance against the harsh government edict. Indeed, most of the significant portraits of tartan-clad gentlemen were commissioned during the ban on tartan.

Opposite: Political campaigns—a depiction of different styles of Highland dress in a scene in which Highland soldiers on the march are companied by camp followers including wives and gillies. This is most likely from the War of the Austrian Succession on the Continent where General Wade's armies were engaged.

that "each Isle differs from the other in their fancy of making Plaids, as to the Stripes in Breadth and Colours. This Humour is as different thro the main Land of the Highlands, in so-far that they who have seen these Places are able, at the first view of a Man's Plaid to guess the Place of his Residence...."[9]

The term "plaid" came from the Scottish word for a woven twill cloth used for garments as well as bed coverings. From there, the word evolved into a Gaelic term for blanket (usually marled or patterned) and commonly was used to describe the garment worn by most men: a long rectangular piece of cloth approximately two yards wide (probably two pieces measuring about thirty inches each, sewn together) and six yards long. By the seventeenth century, it had become known as the "belted plaid" or, in Gaelic, *Feiladh Mor* ("big wrap"), and was distinctive in the way it was worn. According to lore, here is how one put on the *Feiladh Mor:*

> *A belt was laid on the ground and on top of it the plaid was folded length wise into pleats, at right angles to the belt. The wearer then lay down on top of the plaid parallel to the pleats, folded the material on either side of him over the front of his body and fastened the belt around his waist. On standing up, he had a pleated skirt below his waist and a mass of fabric above it. The upper section of the garment could be arranged in a number of ways either as a protection to the upper body or draped to allow the arms complete freedom of movement. At night a tug at the belt converted one's day clothing into bedclothes.*[10]

A number of Scottish dress historians, however, discount the "lying down" method, suggesting that the more streamlined way of dressing might have been to prepleat the plaid in the hand, wrap it around the body, and then secure it with a belt. While less meticulous, this system certainly would have hastened the Highlander's spring into action.

Prior to the sixteenth century, tartan as we would know it today did not exist in Scotland. Certainly checked and striped fabrics and vegetable-dyed wools were used. In later sixteenth-century descriptions of Highland dress, there are numerous allusions to striped or "marlit" (checkered or patterned) plaids. And plaids and mantles were worn over shirts, with the legs left bare. As Hugh Cheape has observed:

it is only in the sixteenth century that evidence for tartan itself becomes plentiful, though it is not specific enough to identify patterns or setts…. By about 1600 it is clear that "tartan" describes a woolen cloth woven in stripes of color. And it was not until the late seventeenth or early eighteenth century that any uniformity was adopted by family, clan, or district.[11]

One of the earliest written documents involving the use of tartan in its modern context is an entry, from 1538, in the Treasurer's Accounts of James V that cites the purchase of "three elnes [a weaver's measure equaling about forty-five inches] Helande Tertane to be hoiss [hose] to the Kingis Grace …" At this point in history, the concepts *Helande* (Highland) and *tertane* (tartan) are inseparable: The Highlands are culturally and topographically different from the rest of Scotland. Craggy and inhospitable, the Highlands were settled by the Picts and ancient Celts in the seventh century C.E. who later formed larger tribes with the Scotti of Ulster. While Scottish Lowlanders based their feudal system on the European model, spoke English, and dressed like the English, the Highlanders

formed their own clan system, retained their Gaelic language, and developed their own distinctive mode of dress.[12]

According to George Buchanan, an historian who wrote *Rerum Scoticoruom Historia* in 1582, the Highlanders were not only noted for their fondness of color but also for their sophisticated recognition of how a subtly shaded tartan could be used as camouflage:

They delight in variegated garments, especially striped, and their favorite colours are purple and blue. Their ancestors wore plaids of many different colours and numbers still retain this custom, but the majority, now, in their dress, prefer a dark brown, imitating nearly the leaves of heather; than when lying upon the heath in the day, they may not be discovered by the appearance of their clothes.[13]

By the onset of the sixteenth century, tartan was considered a valuable rural business in the Highlands, and its value as a commodity started to appear in recorded deeds. For example, there is a record from 1596 in which a Campbell father granted his son a parcel of land for cash and a cloak of beautifully hued *breacan* (another Gaelic word for "marled" or

tartan-patterned). And we know that the tartan trade most assuredly was booming because the "burgesses of the Royal Burgh of Inverness were constantly trying to punish people for infringing their monopoly of dealing in them."[14] The town's inventories at this time included frequent mentions of Highland hose, tartan plaids, and Highland trews, or close-fitting plaid leggings.

When John Taylor, the Thames waterman and self-styled "Kings Water Poet" visited the Braes of Mar in 1618, he takes note of the habits, or garb, of a hunting party:

> ... all and every man in generall, in one habit, as if Licurgus had been there and made lawes of equality. For once in the yeere, which is whole moneth of August, and sometimes part of September, many of the nobility and gentry of the kingdome (for their pleasure) doe some into these Highland countries to hunt, where they doe conforme themselves to the habite of the Highland men who for the most part, speake nothing but Irish; and in former time were those people which were called the "Red-shanks." Their habite is shooes with but one sole apiece; stockings

> (which they call short hose) made of a warm stuff of divers colours, which they call tartane. As for breeches, many of them, nor their forefathers, never wore any, but a jerkin of the same stuff that their hose is of, their garters being bands or wreathes of hay or straw, with a plaed about their shoulders, which is a mantle of divers colours, much finer and lighter stuffe than their hose, with blue flat caps on their heads.[15]

Tartan also found a place on the battlefield, where Highlanders skirmished with neighbors and asserted their skill at war craft. Quick, aggressive, and equipped with light weaponry, the Highland Charge became a model for military tactics, and the Charge's successes strongly affected the esteem in which Highland soldiers were held.[16]

In battle, contingents could be identified by their glorious tartan patterns. James Philip, in his epic poem the *Grameid*, describes the vivid visual impact of the clans at the Battle of Killiecrankie in 1689: "Glengarry's men were in scarlet hose and plaids crossed with a purple stripe; Lochiel was in a coat of

Opposite: Three details of men in tartan. From left to right: Patrick Grant by Colvin Smith (1820s); George IV by Sir David Wilkie (1820s), and John Campbell, Lord Glenorchy by Enoch Seeman (1720s).

three colours, the plaid worn by MacNeil of Barra rivalled the rainbow."

The Highlanders wore their plaids "kilted," that is, pleated above the knee, and their stockings were woven of the same fabric. If they wore leg coverings (as clan chieftains did for heavy weather or when on horseback), they slipped on form-fitting leggings with integral feet called *triubhas* (or "trews" in English), cut on the bias for greater flexibility and usually worn with garters below the knee. (According to Col. Philip Halford-McLeod, British Army Careers Liaison Officer, "they [trews] are the devil to put on and the devil to take off, so many a wearer must have gone to bed with his socks on."[17]) Distinguishing them from their Lowland neighbors, the trews obviously did not resemble other trousers and were a source of pride for the Highlanders.

Women, too, wore the plaid, but not in the same mode as men. Martin Martin, described Highland women as adorning themselves with a large shawl (or "screen," as it was called in English at the time; in Gaelic it was referred to as an *earasaid* or arisaid, in its anglicized form), woven with black, blue, and red plaid stripes on a white field. This garment, which stretched from head to toe, was draped over the head, and covered the face on both sides to provide modesty (although, ironically, by framing the wearer's face, it flattered her). The *earasaid* could be fastened on the breast with a buckle made of silver or brass, according to the quality of the person, or gathered up over the arm. Underneath, one's sleeves might be of scarlet cloth trimmed in gold lace, and one's head might be adorned with a *breid caol*, a narrow kerchief worn by married women, or a *stiom*, a ribbon for an unmarried girl.[18]

The contemporary men's garment known as the kilt is essentially the lower half of the belted plaid with the back pleats cinched. The kilt is thought to have been invented in the 1730s by an English Quaker named Thomas Rawlinson, who owned an iron-smelting foundry in the Highlands. According to legend, Rawlinson apparently found the belted plaids of his

Opposite: A Highland regiment, circa 1910. William Jones Company of the 236th Regiment illustrates the regular Black Watch (the Government Pattern) and variations of the theme created by overchecks (thin stripes of additional color woven into the tartan) to indicate a particular regiment.

Below: Tartan dandy—a reproduction of a Jacobite print of a chieftain (1714) from the Sobieski-Stuarts' colorful tome *The Costume of the Clans.* While extravagant in figure, the costume—a vividly colored jacket, waistcoat, bonnet with feather, and tailored hose—was considered both popular and credible.

Pl. XII.

Highland employees cumbersome on the job, and had a tailor turn the garment into what amounted to a skirt, making it more efficient for his workers. Despite this account, there is no absolute proof that Rawlinson "invented" the kilt; it is entirely possible that the style evolved through adaptations made by the employees themselves. The result was the *felie beg* (also written as "philibeg"or "filabeg" in English), which became hugely popular and, within a short span of time, replaced the bulkier belted plaid throughout the Highlands and in the northern reaches of the Lowlands as well.

TARTAN TAKES ON A POLITICAL STRIPE

The late sixteenth and early seventeenth centuries gave rise to enormous social change in Gaelic society, including changes in contemporary dress styles, and improved economic well-being in the Highlands, partially as a result of the development of the cattle trade. Newly built viable roads opened up the Highlands to neighboring areas and interested and literate tourists who were enchanted by tales of the exploits of the region's exotic denizens. In addition, religious, commercial, and political rivalries fueled period-ic battles, and in this broader, bloodier context, a new image was conceived: the tartan-clad warrior/hero.

The bard, or poet, had heretofore focused on praising the clans. But now he assumed a broader, national point of view, creating powerful nationalistic propaganda. Their songs rang with political import, and the word "tartan" (or *breacan* in Gaelic) became a potent symbol of dignity and nobility.[19]

With the Civil War (1644–50) in which the English parliament, led by Oliver Cromwell, asserted its power over the monarch for the first time and the ultimate exile of the Stuart kings, the clans aligned themselves with the Whigs or Tories, or the Covenanters or Roman Catholics. The Scottish Reformation had begun in the Lowlands, but achieved only partial success in the Gaelic-speaking Highlands which remained a strong pocket of Catholicism. There was widespread suspicion of Catholics among Protestants in both Scotland and England, as they were seen as potentially disloyal and easily recruited as allies by those enemy nations in Europe, largely still loyal to Rome. This divide was to be exacerbated when Catholic Highland loyalty threw itself behind the Jacobite cause, when the Stuart king James VII and II reverted to Catholicism and was deposed in favor of the Protestant grandchildren of

Curiously enough, in earlier times, a number of prohibitions prevented women from wearing plaid. For example, in 1580, the wearing of plaid outdoors "by any Burgess of Guild or Guild craftsman, or by their wives or daughters, unless the latter were prepared to be taken for loose women or 'suspected persons'" was forbidden—under a penalty of forty shillings—in Aberdeen. In Glasgow it was ordained that women no longer could cover their heads with plaids during the sermon after some plaid-wearing women were caught sleeping. The matter became so serious at the Kirk Session in Monefieth that church officials agreed to purchase "ane pynt of tar to put upon the women that held the plaid about their head in church," as John Telfer Dunbar cites in his *History of Highland Dress*.

Charles I, William and Mary of Orange (at the invitation of senior English parliamentarians) during the Glorious Revolution, marking the beginning of Britain's constitutional monarchy.

Highlanders who had become involved in national politics were recruited into the armed conflicts that arose in Britain and Continental Europe. From 1639 on, they were inducted into the cause of the Covenanters (a popularly supported Scottish group who advocated Presbyterianism over Episcopal church governance imposed by the Crown), Royalist risings, and assorted Jacobite battles in support of the exiled Stuart king. (The Jacobites, many from the Highlands region, continued to be a threat to the English government for the next seventy years even though they were not able to crown a Stuart heir.) When the Act of Union took place in 1707, uniting Scotland and England under a British parliament, it banded together Highlanders, Jacobites, and Lowlanders in a wave of joint opposition.

A strong nationalistic Scottish sentiment was taking form, and the emergence of tartan as a potent symbol of this sentiment quickly developed. Sir Walter Scott commented years later that "I have been told, and believed until now, that the use of tartans was never general in [all of] Scotland until the union, with the detestation of that measure [the Act of Union], led it to be adopted as the National colour and the ladies all affected tartan screens."

With the rise of patriotism, tartans became brighter and bolder, highlighting the wearer's fealty to the exiled James VII and II (of Scotland and England respectively), the "king over the water." (The exiled James was called so for being installed, across the English Channel, in France where he was protected by Louis XIV.) Resentment against the Crown, festering in both the Highlands and the Lowlands, erupted in bloody riots and unsuccessful Jacobite risings protesting the Union. The following contemporary account of the rising of 1715 provides a snapshot of Highlanders in battle against the British military:

The Highlanders' cloaths are composed of two short vest, the one above reaching only to their waste, the other about six inches longer; short stockings which reaches not quite to the knee and no breetches; but above all they have another piece of the same stuff of about six yards long which they tie about them in such a manner that it covers their thighs and all their body when they please, but commonly it's fixed on their left shoulder, and leaves their right arm free. This kind of mantel they throw away when they are ready

to engage, to be lighter and less encumber'd, and if they are beat it remains in the field, as happened to our left wing, who having lost that part of their cloaths which protects them most from the cold and which likewise serves them for bedcloaths, could not resist the violent cold of the season.[20]

Ever watchful of the Jacobite threat, the British government took steps to undermine the Highland way of life, passing the mildly enforced Disarming Acts (in 1716 and 1725) and discouraging the use of Gaelic. The Crown also attempted to dissuade the clans from practicing their Catholic or Episcopal faiths, encouraging them to adopt Presbyterianism instead. But over the next couple of decades, the Jacobites—who had been simmering and waiting for their chance to rise up in an effort to install the successors of James VII to power—made several ill-fated bids in what they imagined to be a fulfillment of an ancient Celtic prophecy. Unfortunately, hindsight suggests that in many of these efforts European monarchs like Louis XV stoked Jacobite zeal to reinstall a Stuart in ploys that, while doomed for failure, would serve as diversionary tactics to hinder the English military from waging war against their own nation's forces. With little military commitment or cost, such monarchs sacrificed Jacobite blood to advance their own national interests. In addition, European privateers—essentially government-sponsored pirates that attacked enemy vessels—supported Jacobite causes that would divert Britain from protecting her merchant vessels, thereby improving the chances for lucrative pillaging. One example of this political maneuvering occurred during the 1745 Jacobite campaign that effectively crushed hopes for a future Stuart king.

The devastating Rising of 1745, in fact, began in 1744, when Louis XV—whose nation was engaged in conflict with Britain—enlisted the aid of Prince Charles Edward Stuart (known as "Bonnie Prince Charlie") in a plan to unseat the anti-French Hanoverian king of Britain. The Stuart prince, grandson of James VII, was eager to supplant the king and agreed to invade England with his own troops, whereupon the French would follow with a fleet. Stormy weather, however, forced them to abandon their plans.

The French then indefinitely delayed the invasion, and the increasingly frustrated Charlie decided to force a move by staging a rebellion on British soil that would in turn oblige the French allies to support his troops. Against all advice, Charlie, with a handful of men, landed in the western Highlands in the summer of 1745.

The prince, who sometime earlier had been presented with a gift of Highland dress by Jacobite supporters, adopted the colorful dress for himself and as a uniform for his army. This act of supreme foresight gave his troops a distinctive character and reinforced the notion of tartan as a symbol of Jacobitism. The prince's faith in the symbolic value of the plaid did not go unheralded: Gaelic poets, in their songs, dwelled repeatedly on the prince's impressive physical appearance and that of his soldiers in their array of "bonnet blue and tartan plaid" and "tartan trews." [21]

The ambitious twenty-four-year-old Charlie, though ill-prepared and woefully understaffed, met with spectacular early victory. Backed by an army of about 2,500 Jacobite loyalists, he took the city of Edinburgh and routed the government forces at Prestonpans. The British forces, lacking regiments that were otherwise engaged in European skirmishes and underestimating the unpopularity of their government in Scotland, were hard put to defend themselves. By autumn, though, when the now overconfident prince decided to invade England itself, the government forces had regrouped, calling soldiers back from other European theaters of war.

The odds now were stacked against the Jacobites, and the prince and his men retreated to Scotland, pursued by superior British government troops. Plagued by bankruptcy and short on arms, Bonnie Prince Charlie made the fateful decision to turn and engage in battle on Culloden Moor outside Inverness—an open site unfavorable to the guerrilla-war style tactics of the Highlanders and one that provided a tactical advantage for the government troops. The Duke of Cumberland (the son of the Hanoverian king) struck the following morning with heavy artillery to which the ill-equipped, exhausted Highlanders could not begin to meet their advance.

The Battle of Culloden, on April 16, 1746, was a total

The *BATTLE*

This View of the Glorious Victory obtained over the Rebels, Shews His MAJESTIES Army commanded by His Roya
Body of Reserve, composed of Four – Part of the Highland Army is here represented as furiously attempting wit
mets of Barrels & Munros intrepid Regiments. The right wing of the Rebels being cover'd by a stone Wall, Ke
put them into immediate confusion. Kingstons Horse wheel'd off at the same time by the right of y. Kin

Published 1.ˢᵗ November

CULLODEN April 16, 1746.

...ness the Duke of CUMBERLAND, drawn up in three Lines; the Front consisting of Six Battallions of Foot, the Second of Five, the Third was
...ds & Targets to break in upon the left of the Dukes Front Line, where their Rashness met with its deserved chastisement from the Fire an...
...ham's Dragoons under Hawley & Bland, are describ'd as passing through a breach that had been made for them in it, to attack the rear...
...s & falling on the left of the Rebels met our Dragoons in their Center, on which began the total rout of these disturbers of the Publick Repos...

LAURIE & WHITTLE, 53 Fleet Street, London.

catastrophe and "effectively the end of the Jacobite rising and the prelude to a massive military, judicial, and political assault on the clan society which had spawned Stewart subversion."[22] After heavy losses, the prince's troops reassembled at Ruthven, where Charlie persuaded them to seek their own safety. The prince himself hid with Jacobite sympathizers, often dressed in the garb of a maidservant, and finally escaped to France, leaving Scotland tragically for the last time.

After the defeat of the Jacobite uprising at Culloden, the victorious Duke of Cumberland (bitterly known to the Jacobites as "The Butcher"), commander in chief of the British army, dictated a savage policy of brutality and destruction wherein "hundreds of Highlanders were shot, bayoneted, or where it was convenient, burned alive."[23] Legislation was enacted to dismiss the feudal powers of the great landowners of the Highlands and to abolish the Heritable Jurisdictions that had enabled the chiefs to hold power over their clansmen.

In some ways, though, the most devastating blow to Highlanders was still to come. Government politics reflected a firm conviction that clanship and Highland garb should be destroyed, and accordingly, the draconian Proscription Act of 1746 was imposed. "According to its title," observes historian Fitzroy Maclean, "'An Act

for the more effectual Disarming of the Highlands in Scotland, and for more effectual securing the peace of the said Highlands, and for restraining the use of the Highland dress, & etc.,' the purpose is self-evident and significant in so far as tartan and Highland dress . . . had come to be regarded as an outward and visible manifestation of lawlessness, political treachery, Jacobitism, and continuing loyalty to the Stuart dynasty in exile."[24] The wording of the repressive act was severe and heart-rending:

That from and after the first day of August, One thousand and seven hundred and forty seven no man or boy within that part of Great Britain called Scotland, shall, on any pretext whatever, wear or put on the clothes commonly called Highland clothes, (that is to say) the Plaid, Philabeg, or little Kilts, Trowse, Shoulder-belts, or any part whatever of what peculiarly belongs to the Highland Garb; and that no tartan or party-coloured plaid or stuff shall be used for Great Coats of upper coats, and if any such person shall presume after the said first day of August, to wear or put on the aforesaid garments or any part of them, every such person so offending … shall suffer imprisonment, without Bail, during the Space of Six Months, and no longer;… and being convicted for a second Offence … shall be liable to be transported to any of

His Majesty's plantations beyond the seas, there to remain for the space of seven years.[25]

The bagpipes, the Highlanders' wailing call to battle, were also banned, as the Duke of Cumberland deemed them to be "an instrument of war."

In the following patriotic verse, penned sometime in the 1740s, poet Alexander MacDonald sums up the sentiment of the defeated and "defrocked" Jacobites, using "the plaid" as a symbol for Scottish nationhood:

Better for me is the proud plaid
Around my shoulder and put under my arm
Better than though I would get a coat
Of the best cloth that comes from England.[26]

The banning of the "rebellious and savage" Highland costume provoked deep resentment and indignation, but even Sir Walter Scott admitted "there was knowledge of mankind in the prohibition, since it divested the Highlanders of a dress which was closely in association with their habits of Clanship and of war." Historian Christian Hesketh reported that during the proscription period "trousers were so unpopular among the clansmen, that for long journeys, rather than put them on, they preferred to hang them over their shoulders, and wear instead a makeshift skirt (made of anything but tartan) or the forbidden *philabeg*, stitched down the middle."[27]

As it turned out, "[T]he Act applied only to Scotland and tartan might from time to time be seen in England, such as miniature portraits of Prince Charlie in tartan or the popular line of 'Jacobite' wine glasses with enamel portraits. Tartan had, of course, become inescapably a political symbol and the statute reflected how effectively it had been used by Prince Charles Edward."[28] While tartan could not be flaunted in public by men, the Jacobite ladies (who were not included in the proscription) found ways to skirt the rules. Ramsay of Ochertyre, looking back in the late eighteenth century over more than a generation, observed that "Jacobite ladies took that method of expressing their attachment to an unfortunate prince.

They used tartans not only in plaids, but in gowns, riding clothes, bed and window curtains, even in shoes and pin-cushions."[29]

Another subtle way of preserving tartan and all it represented was taken up by some of the leading noblemen of the day. Most of the great eighteenth-century tartan portraits, featuring their subjects garbed in full Highland dress, were painted during the proscription period and constituted, in effect, an act of plaided protest against the British government. Some subjects even went as far as to have themselves depicted in classical mode, draped in plaid as though it were a toga. The Highlander was beginning to morph into "a heroic and classical figure, the legatee of primitive virtues."[30]

The Act of Proscription stood on the statute books for thirty-five years, during which time Highland life almost completely crumbled. Ironically, only in the armed forces could tartan be worn in Scotland during this period and, as a result, it was the Highland regi-

ments that kept the manufacture of tartan alive.

Since 1725 the government had raised independent companies that included Highlanders entrusted to investigate any suspicious Jacobite action. In 1739 these were formed into regiments and were issued a uniform tartan of the "government pattern" in a green, blue, and black check. The forty-second regiment, called the "Black Watch" for their nightly watch to guard against cattle theft, was one such company. The Black Watch tartan became the standard military pattern.

When other regiments were raised, such as the Gordon Highlanders or the Seaforth, they distinguished themselves by adding a different colored overstripe (a thin line of color in warp and weft, usually red, white, or yellow) to the Black Watch. Later, in 1793, the Cameron Highlanders established a tartan of their own, eschewing the Cameron tartan whose red hue was not thought to harmonize with the scarlet "coatee," or close-fitting military tailcoat, that they wore. The Cameron Highlanders substituted a McDonald tartan

embellished with a yellow stripe borrowed from Cameron. Some historians believe that the notion of differentiation of tartan by clans might have evolved from this desire to distinguish one Highland regiment uniform from another. Certainly, its classification for military use laid the groundwork for many subsequent designs and the movement toward uniformity.

Although the use of tartan uniforms for the Highland regiments in the eighteenth century was meant to popularize those regiments in Scotland, it had the effect of popularizing tartan itself and maintaining and strengthening the idea of group significance attached to patterns. Tartan researcher Donald C. Stewart expressed it thusly:

For it is doubtful whether the traditionalism of the Gael would have sufficed effectively to revive the kilt after its long suppression; but when the Highland regiments proved themselves among the finest fighting material in

the British Army, so that the Scottish nobility sought the honour of command in them, what might have come to be regarded as the barbarous if picturesque dress of a bygone age remained to acquire an aura of military glory.[31]

Apart from the Highlanders' impressive service in the British military, a number of other forces were at work in the latter part of the eighteenth century to shift the public image of the Highlands. One of the first took place in 1782, when the Marquis of Graham, later the Duke of Montrose, introduced a bill in parliament to repeal the Proscription Act, which produced joy in some quarters of Scotland.

The beloved Gaelic poet Duncan Ban McIntyre expressed the feelings of his countrymen in his "Song to the Highland Garb":

We have assumed the suit
That is lightsome and fitting for us
The belted plaid in its pleats…

Left: Curious Parisians attempt to find out what Scottish soldiers wear beneath their kilts.

According to Anne Sutton and Richard Carr, authors of *Tartans, Their Art and History*, "Philip Jennings Clerke said he would oppose the Bill [to repeal the Proscription Act] when brought if it did not confine the Highland dress to the North of the Tweed; for he recollected an innkeeper in Hampshire coming with a complaint before him as a justice of the peace, that four Highland officers were quartered on him, who being brawny handsome fellows, he began to be jealous of his wife, who was not very old, and also fearful for the virtue of his daughters; the Highlanders, being in their own country dress, the females could not keep their eyes off them, which obliged him to take a lodging for them near his house, but far from being able to attend to his business, his whole time was taken up with watching his wife and daughters."

The Gaels will hold up their heads
And they will be hemmed in no more
Those tight fetters have vanished
That made them languid and frail.[32]

Meanwhile, more and more Highland regiments continued to be raised to fight in the Revolutionary War in America and later in the Napoleonic Wars. The military used techniques perfected in the clans—the source of many members of the regiments—to build spirit and establish a new kind of team identity. Tales of the bravery of kilted Highland soldiers in foreign wars were irresistible and served to enhance the image of the tartan-clad hero, restoring to the Highlanders a pride in their ancestry and a desire to preserve Highland dress and the industry that produced it.

When the Allies occupied fashion-conscious Paris after Waterloo in 1815, Sir Walter Scott wrote that "the singular dress of our Highlanders makes them particular objects of attention to the French." Indeed, when the tsar of Russia visited the Élysée Palace in 1835, he demanded to have several soldiers of the Highland regiments paraded before him. Seeming particularly interested in the hose, gaiters, and legs of one Sergeant Thomas Campbell, he pinched the soldier's skin, "thinking I wore something under my kilt" and lifted up the kilts "so that he might not be deceived."[33]

Simultaneous with the new military-inspired appreciation of tartan dress in the latter part of the eighteenth century was a blossoming of literary enthusiasm in the Highlands and the rise, in particular, of Romanticism—the influential artistic and literary movement of the period that countered Neoclassicism with a focus on individual experience and emotion, often through the use of nostalgic or historical subject matter. The publication, in 1760, of a volume titled *Fragments of Ancient Poetry Translated from the Gaelic*, which was purported to be a newly discovered ancient Gaelic narrative epic poem by the third-century bard Ossian, kindled great interest in the hitherto unknown primitive Highland culture. Another volume by the same individual (known as the "Homer of the Highlands"), published five years later, created what was described as a literary explosion of Celtic national pride that resonated throughout Europe. The

Opposite: Two Bairns by Sir John Everett Millais.

author/translator was a schoolmaster named James Macpherson, and "the genuineness of his 'originals' became controversial enough to send two generations of literary inquirers scouring the Highlands and Hebrides for written material in the Gaelic language."[34] The authenticity of these works is still debated, but there is nothing controversial about the positive impact the volumes had on a new appreciation of Gaelic culture.

Tourism swelled during the Romantic period, and writers, antiquarians, geologists, and explorers alike headed for the Highlands. Even the noted English writer Samuel Johnson, who once remarked that the mountains and islands were as foreign as Borneo and Sumatra to the southern inhabitants of Scotland, took his companion James Boswell on a voyage of discovery to the Highlands, and detailed his observations of the "natives'" lives and manners. Finally, the Highlands were becoming fashionable.

A large part of the tartan "revival" also grew out of the establishment, in 1778, of the Highland Society of London (which had been instrumental in the repeal of the Proscription Act) and, six years later, the Highland Society of Scotland. Founded to protect and encourage Highland dress and music as well as Gaelic language and literature, the societies' missions included bolstering economic initiatives in the Highlands. Since the banning of tartan, some of the old dyeing and weaving arts had begun to disappear, and the society appealed to clan chiefs and heads of major families to "furnish as much of the tartan of their clans as will serve to show the patterns." Between 1816 and 1820, about forty samples were submitted, many of them sealed and certified in writing by the clan chiefs. These were sewn into a folio ledger, which is preserved in the society's archives.[35] The association emphasized research and classification of tartan, endowing the subject with a scholarly seriousness heretofore unknown and preserving at least some of the Highland heritage that had been so singularly devastated.

The late Richard Martin, former head of the Costume Institute at the Metropolitan Museum of Art, helmed the first comprehensive tartan exhibition in New York during his tenure at the Fashion Institute of Technology. In the accompanying catalogue, he charted the sea change in the perception of tartan over time. The transformation of Highland tartan dress from a mark of the rebel to an icon of national identity (how tartan was regarded after 1745) was the result of several dynamic changes. Between 1747 and

Right: Mary Cassatt, *Little Girl on a Blue Armchair*, 1878.

1782 (the years of the proscription), tartan was not worn by the common people, who feared official repercussions. At the same time, the Industrial Revolution led to a modernization of dress. As a result, the idea of Highland dress was stored in the collective historical attic, and by the time it was revived in the years leading up to 1822 (the year George IV's plaid-clad appearance in Edinburgh gave tartan his royal approval), it had been forgotten by some two to three generations. When remembered, through a romantic haze, tartan was recalled as the ancient dress of the Highlands, not garb that until recently—the period before 1746 was not so long before George IV's pivotal visit—was standard dress. Martin concluded that "the ban on tartan was hugely successful, but so inimical to a natural historical process that it promoted the violent reassertion of the tartan, sanctioned by a spurious sense of history in the next century."[36]

The influence of two Lowland Scots, the poet and Scottish nationalist Robert Burns and the novelist Sir Walter Scott, also helped situate the Highlands in a newly appealing light and repaired the damaged self-respect resulting from the painful defeat of 1745. Burns's poems stressed tolerance and emphasized human nature with all its virtues and vices, infusing Scots with a new pride. A phenomenally popular author in his day like Burns, Scott was a leading figure in the Romantic movement that transformed European attitudes and aesthetics. He virtually gave back Scotland her history. In his poetry and historical novels, descriptions of the beauties of "Caledonia stern and wild" enthralled a large new audience.

As the Napoleonic Wars had shuttered the gates of Europe to fashionable travelers, a substitute destination was provided by the poems and novels of Sir Walter Scott, which drew attention to scenes of beauty and romance nearer home, idealizing and romanticizing the Scottish Gaels. *The Lady of the Lake* sent tourists to the Trossachs, while *The Lord of the Isles* propelled visitors across the Hebridean seas to the Isles of Skye, Mull, Iona, and Staffa. Within a month of the publication of *Rob Roy* (1817), a stage version was mounted in Edinburgh.[37] The Highlands, which had inspired suspicion and distrust so recently, were beginning to inspire fashion and enormous public interest.

Scott's promotional prowess extended beyond his prolific and influential writings. For example, the Lord Provost of Edinburgh called upon Scott, a Lowlander whom he described as "carried away by his romantic

Celtic fantasies"[38] to organize and helm, with the help of Colonel David Stuart of Garth, founder of the Celtic Society, the extravagant ceremonies for King George IV of England's visit to Edinburgh in 1822.

No monarch had visited Scotland since Charles II in 1651, so George IV's visit in August of 1822 was a reason for playing to the romanticism in the Scottish character that dotes on the pageantry accompanying royalty.[39] Considered something of a dandy in his youth, the king had a liking for Highland dress and was known to have appeared at a fashionable masquerade party as a young man costumed in the kilt. At the time of his official visit to Edinburgh, he was sixty years old, portly, and both personally and politically unpopular, but he brought great enthusiasm to the event. For the reception at Holyrood, his Royal Stewart[40] costume, procured from George Hunter & Co., was a study in opulence, being made of "56m/61yd of satin, 28m/31yd of velvet,

and almost 18m/20yd of cashmere."[41]

As described by one tartan scholar, George IV:

brought to his kingly role a zest and bonhomie which, under the tactful and enthusiastic stage management of Scott made his visit an immense success. With only the briefest preparation, he carried through a strenuous pro-gramme of levees, courts, balls, a military review and civic banquet, and a state procession which enabled him to be seen by thousands of his subjects and brought them, as well as the representatives of the ancient nobility and gentry … into the royal circle.[42]

One of the most extraordinary aspects of the celebra-tion was the fact that Scott ignored Lowland traditions, focusing instead on Gaelic culture—mythical or simply made-up—to create what critics deemed at the time "a plaided panorama." Scott had determined that "the kilt and all its accoutrements, by this time a highly stylized costume which bore little resemblance to the clothing actually worn by the Gaels in the days of clanship, was to be the national dress of Scotland for the purpose of the visit, and planned a number of events for which it was to be obligatory…"[43] Having declared the royal visit to be a "gathering of the Gael," Scott instructed the clan chiefs to "bring half-a-dozen or half-a-score of Clansmen so as to look like an Island Chief as you are. Highlanders are what he (the King) will like most to see."[44]

According to Scottish historian Robert Clyde, by 1822, ironically:

> *Gaeldom had become a minority culture in the process of being marginalized. Yet within a short time, Scott invented for it a bogus tradition that was taken at the time (and still is) to be both ancient and representative of Scotland as a whole. Because Scott had become the acknowledged preserver of Scotland's past, the myths he created were not only believed in but were also assumed to be rooted in antiquity. In presenting the Highland laddie as the archetypical Scot, he not only reduced a country of rich cultural diversity to a one-dimensional caricature, but created a false and highly sanitized picture of Gaeldom.*[45]

It would be no exaggeration to say that the visit of George IV to Edinburgh served as the catalyst for the "romantic rehabilitation of the kilt" and for catapulting tartan—the heretofore humble Highland cloth—into the royal stratosphere. By donning Highland dress, the king gave his seal of approval to tartan as the preferred fashion for Scottish nobility; and, by wearing the Royal Stewart pattern, he conferred upon the tartan instant history, status, and unimpeachable rank (even though it was doubtful the plaid had been in existence for very long). His sartorial choices launched not only a frenzy of interest in tartan, but also one of Scotland's major industries.

Thousands of Highlanders and Lowlanders showed up to the many events orchestrated for George IV's tour, but before stepping out, they had to address a burning question: Which tartan should they wear? The concept of differentiated clan tartans, newly popularized, was codified and developed by canny manufacturers whose only clients for the previous thirty-five years had been the Highland regiments. Since the repeal of the Proscription Act of 1782, these tartan makers saw the prospect of a vast new market. The greatest of these firms was that of William Wilson and Son of Bannockburn, whose copious records are invaluable sources for historians. In business since 1724, Wilson had the foresight to compile an inventory of differentiated

Left: A watercolor of Queen Victoria's sitting room at Balmoral, decorated in different tartans by an unnamed artist in *Leaves from the Journal of Our Life in the Highlands.*

Left: The Balmoral tartan, designed by Victoria's husband, Prince Albert. With its gray background suggesting the Grampian mountains of the Highlands, the sett is based on the Royal Stewart, but woven in this color-way, it is meant to be worn strictly by the royal family.
Opposite: Balmoral Castle, Victoria and Albert's beloved home in the Scottish Highlands (photo from 1937).

clan tartans. With the aim of using the firm's catalogue to urge customers to climb aboard the clan bandwagon, Wilson joined the Highland Society of London, "which threw over their commercial project a cloak or plaid of historic respectability."[46]

Wilson and Son's early records on tartan, dating directly after the repeal of proscription, were somewhat sketchy and, though they included a list of tartans with their associated clans or names, almost none are a clan sett today. It was noted that with weak public demand and scant funds, tartan requests were limited to several of the better-known clan patterns, or as one somewhat nondiscriminating customer said, "The colours I leave to yourself and let them be handsome."[47] Thirty years later, though, the desire for tartan had risen dramatically in anticipation of George IV's visit. Messr. J. Spittal and Son of Edinburgh wrote to Wilson and Son saying, "We are like to be torn to pieces for tartan, the demand is so great we cannot supply our customers."[48] When the royal visit was first anticipated, the Wilson firm worked in tandem with the Highland Society, preparing tartan samples

for the latter to certify as belonging to one clan or another. But apparently, when the king's visit neared, all preparations flew out the window, and emphasis was placed on supply and demand. According to Hugh Trevor-Roper, "Cluny Macpherson, heir to the chief of the clan, was given a tartan labeled 'MacPherson,' but previously having been sold in bulk to a Mr. Kidd to clothe his West Indian slaves, it had been labeled 'Kidd' and before that it had simply been 'No. 155.'"[49]

The "tartanization" of the Scottish capital was a colossal hit with many of Edinburgh's citizenry, but there were some notable exceptions. Sir Walter Scott's own son-in-law, J. G. Lockhart, was particularly disdainful of Highlanders gathered under the command of their clan chiefs in full regalia, calling them a "Celtic hallucination." Later, Lord Macaulay, a Highlander by origin, wrote that he himself did not doubt the antiquity of the Highland dress, but "his historical sense was outraged by the retrospective extensions of these 'striped petticoats' to the civilized races of Scotland," adding that "this absurd modern fashion had reached a

point beyond which it was not easy to proceed." As Trevor-Roper ironically observed of Lockhart, "he underestimated the strength of a hallucination sustained by economic interest."[50]

It should be pointed out that before the Act of Proscription, the upper and middle classes of Scotland often regarded Highland garb as a "badge of servility." But with the blessings of the king, Scots—both Highland and Lowland—began to look upon Highland dress with greater enthusiasm. Twentieth-century Scottish diplomat and writer Fitzroy MacLean wryly noted that the enthusiasm for tartan was not only great but seemingly universal: It was surprising indeed that "a number of normally self-respecting Lowland lairds proudly displayed themselves in Highland costumes which their fathers and grandfathers ... would not willingly have been seen dead in."[51]

Several books were compiled to record the subject of the tartan frenzy that George IV's trip to Edinburgh sparked. James Logan's *The Scottish Gael,* published in 1831, reflected the author's extensive research throughout Scotland and recorded for the first time the existence of fifty-four distinctive tartan patterns that he could authenticate. Logan, like many of his contemporaries, took a highly romanticized view of Scottish history,

and his book motivated just about every manufacturer in Scotland to invent new clan tartans to satisfy the insatiable appetites of their customers.

To further codify tartan and its clan associations, a second, grander reference book appeared in 1842, created by two bearded brothers who claimed, with no particular credentials, to be the legitimate, long-lost grandsons of the beloved Bonnie Prince Charlie. Known as the Sobieski-Stuarts (through family connections to Polish royalty: Princess Clementina Sobieska, granddaughter of Jan Sobiseki III, King of Poland in the late seventeenth century, married Prince James Stuart, the "Old Pretender"), John and Charles Hay Allen were taken up by sympathetic noblemen and allowed to live in the splendor to which they claimed to have been accustomed. Lord Lovat built a house for them at Eilean Aegis, his island estate on the River Glass, near Beauly. Here, they illustrated, compiled, and embellished a volume, classifying an array of clan tartans, impeccably and beautifully detailed, but probably not grounded in historical reality. Containing seventy-five tartan setts, their artistic treatise, published in 1842 and titled *Vestiarium Scoticum,* was alleged to have been taken from a sixteenth-century manuscript, a claim that endowed it with great pedi-

gree. Although its contents were never proven to be authentic, the book was impressive enough to form the basis of a number of clan tartan setts that are still worn today. The volume was succeeded two years later by an even more monumental tome titled *The Costume of the Clans*, which was brilliantly produced, but riddled with fantasy and forgery. The two books were attacked on all sides for their often-flawed accounts, but the Sobieski-Stuarts did succeed in collecting a vast amount of material on the dress, customs, and history of the Highlands at a time when all three were in danger of being forgotten. They also served as authorities for a number of tartans and, just as importantly, enhanced the importance of tartan in the public mind.

If George IV was the first to give a "royal stamp of approval" to the tartan revival, his niece Victoria sealed the deal. Twenty years after the king's visit to Scotland, Victoria and her husband, Prince Albert of Saxe-Coburg-Gotha, made their first trip to the Highlands

where they were received by the Atholl clan, replete with a thousand Campbell-kilted Highlanders, pipers playing, guns firing, and crowds cheering. As the besotted twenty-three-year-old Victoria herself noted in her journal, "it was princely and romantic."[52]

Bolstered by their impressive reception, Victoria and Albert returned again and again to the Highlands and finally, in 1848, stayed at Balmoral Castle for the first time. The queen and her prince bought the estate and worked with a local architect to remodel it in the "Scots Baronial" style. Prince Albert was primarily responsible for designing the interior of the castle, where tartans were juxtaposed with chintzes to create the relaxed informality of a hunting lodge. Albert made great use of the bright red of the Royal Stewart and the green of Hunting Stewart tartans for the carpets, while curtains and upholstery featured the Dress Stewart, with its handsome white background. Even the draperies in the carriages were of Royal Stewart fabric. And in addition to the old tartans, two new ones were

Second from left: John Brown, the personal attendant to Queen Victoria. After the death of her beloved husband, Albert, Victoria spent much of her time at Balmoral and became close friends with her ghillie, John Brown, which became gossip fodder for years to come.
Third from left: Tartan dressing gowns for men and women from the Victorian age. He has on a plaid dressing gown, skull cap, and slippers, and she is wearing an evening dress with lace volans and bertha, as well as a skirt swagged with lace and roses. Hand-colored fashion plate from *La Mode,* July 1841.
Near left: Portrait of Prince Albert.

invented: the "Victoria," which we owe to the queen, and the better-known "Balmoral," of which Prince Albert was the designer. Based on the Royal Stewart, but done in shades of marled gray to represent the rugged peaks of the Highlands, its use is still restricted to members of the royal family.

Victoria and Albert adored the Highlands and chose to spend a substantial amount of time each year at their Scottish home. In so doing, they adopted a host of Highland activities: The queen had always enjoyed dancing and "at Balmoral everybody was encouraged to take part in the reels and country dances that she loved. Even in England the habit persisted, and when balls were given at Windsor or in London, it was not only *mazurkhas* and *gavottes* that were seen, but Scottish dances with their unfamiliar patterns."[53] Victoria loved being attended by pipers or watching the royal children playing in kilts, and Prince Albert adored watching the Highland games.

During the period that Victoria and her family savored the joys of Balmoral, access to the area became far easier: New roads were constructed, and railways and shipping services connected the Highlands to the rest of the world. Visitors flocked to Scotland, and a burgeoning tourist souvenir trade was born. According to author Iain Zaczek, "Suddenly tartan designs were no longer confined to woven materials, but could be found on every imaginable form of knick-knack—from tea caddies and spectacle cases to cheap jewelry and plates. Highlandism had found a powerful commercial outlet … one that has continued to thrive to the present day."[54]

FASHION

"All cultures tap into the power, real or imagined, of dress."[1]

—Cathy Newman, National Geographic's *Fashion*

While George IV set the stage for tartan as "national dress" for the Scottish nobility, Victoria and Albert's "cult of the Highlands" turned dress into fashion. The Victorian obsession with etiquette dictated that different styles of dress be worn for day and evening, thereby creating a need for new styles of clothing. Accompanying this increased demand was the development of chemical aniline dyes that made vibrant new colors possible, which enhanced plaid's possibilities. Thus, in addition to the existing clan setts, specialized tartans were created to suit specific occasions: darker, muted hunting setts to blend with the countryside for daytime and more formal, bright or white-grounded dress setts for those who could afford to dress for dinner. And since the Victorians would observe convention to the grave, black-and-white funeral tartans were designed for mourning.

Opposite: Vivienne Westwood's turban and greatcoat over a miniskirt in her own McStone tartan from "Five Centuries Ago," her autumn/winter 1992–93 collection.

Prior to the nineteenth century, tartan was mainly the province of men, largely because of its ancestral roots in the military. Now, in mid-century, following Victoria's lead, women began to wear it as "fashion," as fabrics became kinder to the touch, with soft Saxony cloth often supplanting the hard, dense twill. Rich, lustrous silks that showed off tartan's colors and patterns beautifully became all the rage, in emulation of the royals. Tartan dresses, shawls, bodices, and sashes became haute couture not only in Scotland but also in Britain, France, and beyond.[2]

A few decades later and with the same passion for the plaid possessed by his predecessors—George IV, Victoria, and Edward VII—Edward, Duke of Windsor, was able to promote tartan by virtue of his royal status, "extending its appeal beyond courtly, aristocratic, and bourgeois circles."[3] By combining his plaids and checks in unusual ways, he made tartan a perennial fixture on the golf course, with his Glen plaid plusfours, and a staple of the Riviera, with his tartan bathing trunks and luxe lounge suits.

To this day, the British royal family's enthusiastic endorsement—and frequent wearing—of tartan has had an enormous influence on its popularity in fashion. By virtue of its royal association, we imbue tartan with all sorts of qualities—class, heritage, comfort, staying power, and authenticity. To some, it symbolizes the breeding that money will never be able to buy.

To others, particularly in England's punk movement in the 1970s and 1980s, tartan was used in subversive ways to express antipathy toward the conservative Anglo-Saxon tradition, its government, and social conformity in general.

Like all fashion, tartan can be construed to embody conflicting impulses and associations; hence, the innocent sexiness of a plaid school uniform or the utility of a tartan skirt that suggests pragmatism and at the same time pedigree. Or consider tartan's exuberant colors that are constrained by boxlike grids or the notion of swagger and subtlety coexisting.

Opposite: The Duke of Windsor's closet at the Mill, France, with tartan pants and kilts perfectly pressed and lined up in regimental order.
Right: Edward VIII as Prince of Wales in his dashing golf duds.

Perhaps tartan's allure resides in its ability to fuse sex and propriety, freedom and restriction, conformity and rebellion, identity and camouflage, luxury and ordinariness, harmony and dissonance, inspiration and aspiration. It appeals to just about everybody, regardless of gender, generation, or geography. No wonder astronaut Alan Bean brought a swatch of tartan with him to the moon!

THE DUKE OF WINDSOR

"Did he have style? The Duke of Windsor had style in every buckle on his kilt, every check of his country suits, in the way he put together sports clothes."
—Diana Vreeland

Of all the things Prince Edward Albert Christian George Andrew Patrick David, born in the last decade of Queen Victoria's reign, inherited from his great-grandmother, his love for tartan was the most memorable. The man best known for abdicating the throne of England for the woman he loved exceeded even Victoria's passion for plaid. His royal status made him a style arbiter not only for his own generation but for generations to come. Credited with making the plaid seem both aspirational and accessible, Edward, in fact, made tartan cool.

As Prince of Wales (and, very briefly, King Edward VIII), the Duke of Windsor was noted for his consummate sartorial savvy, and particularly for infusing his wardrobe

with surprising touches that reflected his lively fashion sensibility. With an unflagging attention to detail, he brought a contemporary dash to his trademark Prince of Wales Glenurquhart checks, ultra-baggy plus-fours, tartan-and-argyle mixes. As an issue of American *Vogue* noted in 1967, "He has ... his own manner of putting things together, contrasting checks with stripes, bold color with bolder color ... all in a hundred combinations of improbable elegance." It has been said that for the duke, style *was* his substance.

The product of an exceedingly formal and rigorous upbringing, the duke favored an elegant but relaxed wardrobe. British fashion editor Suzy Menkes had the opportunity to inspect firsthand the duke's wardrobe and remarked:

> *Not until I unfolded the monogrammed shirts or examined the misty check tweed suits did I realize how studied that style really was. The discreet tab behind the jacket lapel to hold the natty carnation, button hole; the trousers cut high in the waist to emphasize the board-flat stomach; the unlined tweeds as an escape—metaphorical and literal—from the starched shirts, morning dress, and royal court uniforms of what the duke called a "buttoned-up childhood in every sense."*[4]

Consciously (and perhaps self-consciously), the duke's response to his strict upbringing was to go in the opposite direction. According to Katell le Bourhis, former curator of the Costume Institute at the Metropolitan Museum of Art in New York, the duke was "the first man to dress in unstructured clothes with no stiffness or interlining. He picked up things from English country life and turned them into fashion for the city." She dubbed his look "*chic fatigué*"—a kind of easy casual stylishness."[5]

While the Duke of Windsor's style was infinitely more relaxed than that of his royal forebears, his regal ancestry certainly influenced it. His grandfather, Edward VII (or "*le bon boulevardier*," as the Parisians called him), often dressed in tartans and tweeds and was known as a natty dresser despite his girth. "This bright tweeded opulence of my grandfather and his friends, while out shooting at Sandringham, was always a wonder to me as a child," the duke recalled.[6] (It wasn't until the mid-nineteenth century that tartan tweeds and shepherd's plaid began to be used generally for men's trousers. Prior to that time, men's trousers were made only in somber gray and black fabrics.)

In his own book, *Windsor Revisited*, the duke expounded upon the then novel notion of checkered pants:

> *Countless variations were to be played on this shepherd's*

Left: The Duke and Duchess of Windsor dancing at home at the Mill.

plaid pattern. Colours were to be introduced into it, overchecks superimposed upon it. District checks were to be evolved, of which the most famous was—and still is— the Glenurquhart.[7]

(The Glenurquhart check is often referred to as the "Prince of Wales" check.) He continued, explaining that new tartans evolved or were designed not just for Scottish lairds and their families but for their retainers as well. Albert, the Prince Consort, Queen Victoria's husband, designed the Balmoral, adapting it from the Royal Stewart tartan in a black-and-white pattern with a bold red overcheck. Worn by the royal family, the Balmoral tartan also was used both to clothe the employees on the estate and to upholster the chairs in the castle. "When I myself became King," explained the duke, "I introduced it as the tartan for the pipers at Balmoral, who had hitherto worn Royal Stewart."[8]

The duke reminisced about his fondness for tartan: "I have always liked the Highland tartans. In my closets at the Mill [Le Moulin de La Tuilerie, the Windsor home in the Bois de Boulogne on the outskirts of Paris] I still have a number of old kilts, and I wear this comfortable Highland dress for evening. They are of the various tartans which I have a right to wear—Royal Stewart, Hunting Stewart, Rothesay, Lord of the Isles, Balmoral."[9]

He noted that he preferred tartans made with vegetable dyes over those made with chemical ones since their colors, in his opinion, were truer.

The duke indeed doted on his tartan kit. It was noted that during the 1940s, in the sultry heat of July at Cap D'Antibes, while everyone was wearing the coolest, thinnest fabrics imaginable, the duke appeared in full Scottish rig. As his friend Fruity Metcalfe recalled: "He was completely turned out as a Scotch laird about to go stalking. His appearance was magnificent, if indeed a little strange considering the tropical heat."[10]

With the kind of attention to minute detail that made him such an icon of style, he also discourses on the length of kilts, indicating that the kilt lengths he wears are shorter than those of his father and grandfather, whose "decently longer" lengths had been introduced by Prince Albert.

To say that the duke had a predilection for pattern is an understatement. He was fully capable of pairing a black-and-white houndstooth Harris Tweed jacket and waistcoat with a scarlet, green, and yellow plaided Royal Stewart tartan kilt. At times he also piled on a mélange of plaids and checks in shirt, tie, and suit. According to Nicholas Lawford, a friend of the duke's in prewar Paris: "In a world where men tend to look

more and more alike, he seems more than ever endowed with the capacity to look like no one else."[11] More recently, legendary interior designer Mario Buatta, who also shares a love for novel combinations of traditional patterns, wittily summed up the duke's unique influence: "The Duke of Windsor was our style leader. Pattern on pattern on pattern. Who else did that?"

Edward was no less interested in color. "I believe in bright checks for sportsmen," he once wrote, "the louder they are, the better I like them." The duke instructed the tailor who made all of his trousers, H. Harris of New York, to fashion pants in audacious combos such as pink, blue, orange, and white checks. Another pair was ordered in a gutsy lemon, blue, green, and oatmeal plaid. (The duke preferred the London tailors Scholte of Savile Row for his jackets even though his pants were sewn in New York, an arrangement the duchess amusingly referred to as "pants across the sea."[12])

Edward extravagantly employed color and pattern in his wardrobe yet he was positively parsimonious when it came to buying new clothing. His wife once remarked she was somewhat puzzled by the fact that her husband was regarded as a leader of men's fashion since he rarely bought a suit. She used the following anecdote to illustrate his thrift: "Take for instance the tartan dinner suit His Royal Highness wore last night at dinner. According

Left: The designer Ralph Lauren.
Opposite: Ralph Lauren's velvet-collared, brass-buttoned tartan jacket. Arthur Elgort/*Vogue*/© Condé Nast Publications.

to the tailor's marks on the inside pocket, it was made for his father in 1897."[13] The duke admitted that he had the suit altered to fit him and to replace its button fly with a zipper—a change that, he allows, would have horrified his father. A striking Rothesay tartan (red-and-yellow plaid on a dark green background) lounge suit, it was worn by the duke for dinner one evening at Cap D'Antibes. Apparently, one of their dinner guests mentioned the fact to a friend in the men's fashion trade who felt compelled to cable the news to the U.S. Within a few months "tartan had become a popular material for every sort of masculine garment, from dinner jackets and cummerbunds to swimming trunks and beach shorts. Later the craze even extended to luggage."[14]

According to Kerry Taylor, the Sotheby's specialist in London who prepared the 1998 auction of the Windsor estate, "not since his forebear King George IV in the 1820s [who was largely responsible for the soaring resurgence of interest in tartan] had a monarch lavished so much care and expense on his own personal appearance. He bought clothes of the finest quality, but literally expected them to last a lifetime, which, in fairness, many of them did."[15]

RALPH LAUREN

"You don't have to have the country estate, the access to the wilderness. The clothes can be used to create your own world."
—Consolata Boyle, costume designer for *The Queen*

The term "Anglophile" fits the American designer Ralph Lauren like a bespoke suit: there is no greater admirer of aristocratic English life. But while Lauren admits that he is often inspired by Anglo-style, he has added his self-assured stamp to it, not literally re-creating clothes "the way they were," but interpreting them through an idealized American lens, and rethinking them so they look even better than they did the first time around.

Lauren, whose classic taste and sense of elegance was honed by the great Jimmy Stewart and the Cary Grant films of his youth, is the natural heir to the Duke of Windsor's fashion legacy. His precise, but looser tailoring, his understanding of clothes that improve with longevity, his insistence on classic style, not "of-the-moment" fashion are all elements that can be said to have emanated from the duke. The same

Opposite: Sweater and scarf from the Polo holiday 2005 collection.
Right: A chunky lumberjack shirt from Polo fall 1983.
Following pages: Two young girls twirling away in tartan from Ralph Lauren from fall 1998, and a woman wearing Black Watch from Ralph Lauren Black Label 2001.

heritage is the source of his love for tartan and his ability to put together clothes that mix patterns—all of which the duke did brilliantly and seemingly effortlessly—in the best English sporting tradition. As Lauren's biographer Colin McDowell has said:

For Ralph, it was not just the perfection of cut that characterized all the Duke's clothes, even at their most casual; it was the supremely relaxed way in which he wore them. No matter what the occasion, he never looked like a tailor's dummy. The clothes never dominated the man. It is the essence of the Ralph Lauren philosophy of dress."[16]

As an unabashed Anglophile, Lauren recalls how thrilled he was to meet Queen Elizabeth when she visited Bloomingdale's department store during the American Bicentennial in 1976. As she stopped at the Ralph Lauren Polo shop within the sophisticated New York department store, Lauren remembers anxiously wondering "whether she would think we were laying claim to an English heritage by showing so many tartans and tweeds." Instead, the queen assured him that "she was very pleased with what we had done."

In the same vein, when Lauren opened his first Polo

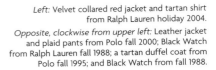

shop in London in 1981, he says he was certain that "people must have thought I was bringing the proverbial 'coals to Newcastle' by supplying the British with something that was basically of their own tradition. But, of course, it wasn't strictly their tradition, but their tradition, done *my* way, the way I *imagined* it should have been done." The shop was a great success and has since been joined in London by another much larger Polo store.

Lauren's eyes twinkle when he speaks about one of his perennial favorites, tartan, which he confesses he has always loved for its beauty, lushness, and lineage, and, maybe most importantly, its timelessness. As he says, "tartans come in and go out with regularity. But when I look at tartan, say, for a new season, I always feel that I'm rediscovering it. Of course, *it* doesn't change. What changes are the different ways we can

look at it. Its appeal is almost endless. That, to me, is why people connect so well with tartan, why it's recognizable to everybody."

The designer's understanding of "the talismanic quality" of authentic old clothes is rooted in the fact that as the youngest of three brothers, he "inherited" hand-me-downs from his older brothers and by the time he got to wear them, they had acquired a patina of experimental credibility, almost like wearing a little "piece of family history."[17] No wonder he could relate to the Duke of Windsor having his father's Rothesay tartan lounge suit retailored to fit him—then wearing it for another forty years!

The philosophy behind Lauren's early women's collections, according to Colin McDowell, was akin to that of the English upper classes. It was:

From left to right: A boy's Black Watch blazer from Polo holiday 2001; Belted tartan jacket from Ralph Lauren fall 1991; Black Watch boots from Ralph Lauren holiday 2001; and a detail of Ralph Lauren's tartans and tweeds from Polo fall 1988.

male dominated, country-oriented and largely indifferent to the shallow seasonal shifts of Paris fashion. If, by definition, fashion is an urban-based cosmopolitan phenomenon, then style is country-based and, throughout history, has almost always been male-led. Upper-class Englishwomen from the thirties through the fifties used their couturiers to provide them with a female equivalent of what their fathers, brothers, and husbands were wearing ... Many of the grandest women in Britain had their country suits cut and "built" by their husband's tailor just as his boot-maker made them sturdy leather brogues ...[18]

This was a philosophy that Ralph Lauren instinctively understood, just as he intuited that style would outdistance fashion for his kind of woman.

Clearly, the backbone of Ralph's style—for both men and women—has been quality—and he has always drawn upon the best the United Kingdom has to offer, choosing his woolens from England, cotton from Lancashire, tweeds from Scotland. But his fashion thinking, while reflecting British heritage and its respect for intrinsic value, is rooted in a modern American sensibility. He commented recently:

I've always liked the idea of taking the past and reinventing it to my own standards. [In 2006] I was asked to design new uniforms for the Wimbledon Tennis Championship officials. So I immediately checked out the Wimbledon archives, assuming we'd find great old photographs of the golden days of the sport. But it turned out, that was not the case: the old uniforms lacked uniformity—they were not the impeccable blazers and flannels that I had imagined, but a mixed bag of mismatched clothing. What we "reinvented" had never actually been there at all: it was simply the way I imagined it might have been.

Left: Inspired by Tudor portraiture, Vivienne Westwood's velvet-collared beetle jacket and miniskirt in the designer's own McBrick tartan.
Right: Viva Viv—Dame Vivienne Westwood at an after-party for her spring 2002 collection.

VIVIENNE WESTWOOD

"You have a much better life if you wear impressive clothes." —Vivienne Westwood

There is nothing like Dame Vivienne Westwood whose often transgressive work with tartan has changed our perception of the plaid. When author Cathy Newman interviewed the designer for her book *Fashion* she recorded her visual impression in an unforgettable snapshot:

> *She wears a pair of beaded fur moccasins, plaid knee-highs (one has a run in it) and a sleeveless green dress with shoulders that slip low enough to show a ruby red bra strap. To add to the vibrating patterns in the room, she sits in a plaid upholstered chair on a plaid rug—plaids being a Westwood trademark—while an armchair upholstered in yet a third plaid stands in the corner of her office …* [19]

Iconoclast from the outset, Vivienne Westwood introduced her distinctive notion of nonconformity to fashion design, and subsequently to tartan, by infusing her art with a rebellious spirit. Raised in the north of England in a working-class family, she hitched her creative star early on to Malcolm McLaren, whose antiauthoritarian ethos earned him a leading role in London's punk movement and the role of manager of the band the Sex Pistols. McLaren was drawn to anarchy and rock 'n' roll, and together he and Westwood created ways to express themselves by politicizing the clothes they made.

They improvised brilliant antifashion style by ripping, cutting, and pinning clothes, and borrowing details from Teddy boys and rockers, bikers and sex fetishists that brought to their King's Road boutique an unusual clientele: prostitutes and voyeurs along with young protopunk kids. Their shop (which went by such assorted provocative names as "Sex," "Seditionaries,"

and "World's End," its current moniker) was described by McLaren as "a haven for the disenfranchised, which, in turn, helped to create the phenomenon known as punk rock."[20] McLaren and Westwood understood, as Peter York has said, that "The point of this stylistic extremism is simple: it polarizes. Through alienation, it creates a sense of community. Identity through outrage."[21]

By the 1980s Westwood had become more engaged in fashion than music, and her own style began to crystallize, as Claire Wilcox, Westwood's biographer and a leading expert on contemporary fashion has said—"typified by an exactitude, interest in cut and form, exaggeration and restriction—elements that have characterized her work ever since."[22]

In fact, Westwood's work is quintessentially English in that it possesses the dichotomous nature of London fashion itself. She is one of the few designers to assert that tailoring is the basis of her collection, just as it is the basis of her country's vaunted reputation for clothing. While often outrageous, her outfits inspired by punks, pirates, and plaid-clad noblemen are also very precise.

When Westwood turned to historical dress for inspiration, she began to rework it to make it her own. For her landmark autumn/winter 1987–88 collection she

dubbed "Harris Tweed," Westwood mined the vast store of homegrown British fabrics, gently but irreverently parodying establishment styles—the clothes of boarding schools, royalty, and country wear. Her ambivalence toward the aristocracy is expressed by employing its status symbols on her clothing with the implication that it is justifiable to highjack tradition to gain attention: Her clothes are always geared to focusing attention on the wearer.

Using pictorial tradition as inspiration and design source, for her autumn/winter 1990–91 collection titled "Portrait"—which married the notion of French aristocratic dress with English tailoring and charm—Westwood played with opulent lace, velvet, tartan, tweed, linen, and satin, developing whimsical and witty send-ups of nineteenth-century style. She even invented her own tongue-in-cheek tartan setts like "McBrick," which was fashioned after the colors of London's streets. She explained at the time that she had "taken the vocabulary of royalty—the traditional British symbols and used it to her own advantage—utilizing the conventional to make something unorthodox."[23]

While tartan had been incorporated in much of Westwood's work up to this point, it was with her collection "Anglomania" (fall/winter 1993–94) that she

demonstrated her enthrallment with English and Scottish traditions, creating clever, over-the-top takes on tartan minikilt-clad tarts and English gentlewomen. Rebecca Arnold writes on the bravado of Westwood's approach to tartan, which she has used more successfully than almost any other designer:

> Her designs demand a present that is as dramatic and purposeful as that inhabited by, for example, MacDonnell of Glengarry, painted by Raeburn [see page 79, upper left] in the late eighteenth century, in what was itself a wistful mythology of Scottish identity. For Westwood, women can cut just such a dashing and heroic figure as men, in clothes that are just as much about constructing and idealized, theatricalized femininity as they are about representing national identity.[24]

Westwood also has an intuitive understanding of coquetry: Her clothes ooze with sexual charge. She is celebrated for bosoms spilling from tight corseted waists and for satirical T-shirts printed with feminine cleavage. If, as wisdom holds that "the brighter the plumage, the more successful the bird at mating," Westwood is on to something critical to fashion: that, as the British psychologist J. C. Flugel has said, "of all the motives for wearing clothes, those connected with the sexual life have a predominant position."[25]

To further illuminate Westwood's aesthetic, Arnold compares the visual aspects of Westwood's work with Swagger portraiture—a European and British style of painting, popular during the seventeenth to nineteenth centuries—in which subjects are depicted in grand, opulent, often sexy terms. Arnold suggests (per the words of Nicholas Serota, curator and director of the

Tate Museum) that "bombast, glamour, and dressing-up, and not a little unconscious humor" prevails.[26] The obvious swagger of a tartan ensemble from her autumn/winter 1994–95 "On Liberty" collection displayed many of her design concerns. As Arnold describes:

Its bright red cloth drew attention to the intricate tailoring of both the jacket, complete with nineteenth-century puffs at the shoulder, and the asymmetry of the dress's hem. It also served to emphasize the neatly padded bustle strapped across the model's bottom. The outfit clearly demonstrates her attachment to the idea of "dressing-up," masquerading in your clothes, defying the social or cultural status that may have been allotted to you, and re-forming your body in clothes that aspire to create a new culture.[27]

While Westwood's paradoxical dressing—part rigorous design, part outrageous romp—has thrived among fashionistas in the U.K., U.S., and Europe, it is interesting to note that she has enjoyed her greatest commercial success in Japan. Ironically, it is here that "her

eccentric and markedly English work signifying an energy and anticorporate ideal is attractive to a generation of consumers frustrated by the conformity expected by the Japanese system."[28]

In the end, it would seem that Westwood, who started out as a teacher, is educating us about Englishness and undeniably about class. As Arnold points out, "She willfully transgresses fixed ideas of the gender, class, ethnicity and sexuality that the Establishment stands for ... giving her the opportunity to exploit the power of visual revolt."[29]

In appreciation for her ingenious and significant contributions to English fashion, H.M. Queen Elizabeth II conferred both the prestigious OBE (Order of the British Empire) in 1992 and a DBE (Dames Commander of the Order of the British Empire) in 2006 for services to fashion. After each pomp-filled ceremony, in what could only be dubbed classic Westwood style, she celebrated by twirling in a full tartan skirt sans underwear outside Buckingham Palace.

BURBERRY

"Yes, there's the allure of history and England and all that. But . . . there's something transcendent about the brand. It crosses genders and generations and boundaries. People put it on and make 'Burberry' their own."

—Rose Marie Bravo

In 1879 when Thomas Burberry invented a weather-proof cloth that could breathe and keep its cool under the most inclement conditions, he created the foundation of a business that went on to serve men everywhere, from the trenches of World War I to the windswept polar regions of Antarctica. Burberry fashioned a popular coat—called "the gabardine" after the fabric he had patented—which later became known by the name of its maker when King Edward VII got into the habit of saying, "Give me my Burberry."

Thomas Burberry opened his first shop in Basingstoke, Hampshire, in 1856 to outfit the local gentry in functional gear for sport. So, when his company was commissioned by the British War Office to adapt its earlier officer's coat for combat in the trenches, functional coats were just a few alterations away. For example, D-rings were added to the belts to secure satchels holding grenades, maps, and flasks, and epaulettes held straps for satchels, binoculars, and gas masks. This style set the template for what would become one of the design classics of all time: the trench coat.

In 1924, not long after the war and with absolutely no fanfare, Burberry added its trademark check fabric in the now-famous camel, black, red, and white pattern to line the trench coat. In a case of typical British understatement, the check remained there, barely noticed, for the next fifty years.

Meanwhile, the Thomas Burberry Company grew and prospered, catering to the leisure classes of the "smart set" of the 1920s and 1930s with outfits for golf, grouse shooting, trout fishing, riding, cycling, tennis, archery, skiing, skating, and motorcycling, many of which were designed for both men and women.

When World War II broke out, Burberry produced weatherproofs for all divisions of the services. After the war, when a more relaxed urban style emerged, Burberry was at the vanguard. During the 1950s and

Left: Taking a raincheck—Burberry's autumn/winter 2006 catwalk show in Milan.

Following pages: Kate Moss entrenched in insouciance and the Burberry style. Only a glimpse of the firm's iconic check is shown on the coat lining and a shoe, but it immediately identifies the brand.

1960s, their trench coats became Hollywood legends along with the stars who wore them: Humphrey Bogart in *Casablanca*, Audrey Hepburn in *Breakfast at Tiffany's*, and Peter Sellers in the *Pink Panther* films.

It was not until 1972, however, that the iconic check "came out" for the first time, after Burberry was chosen as one of the outfitters for the British Olympic women's equestrian team. As the team members were about to board their plane for Tokyo, someone had the brilliant idea of folding their Burberry trench coats inside out over their arms, with the tartan lining in full view of the cameras. In a flash, the check took center stage, emblematic not only of Burberry but also of Great Britain, tradition, equestrian chic, and exclusivity. Almost overnight the Burberry check became an international status symbol; the lining was on its way to becoming a logo.

Burberry continued to evolve its classic style, becoming an important part of the British export industry as it expanded its product and worldwide distribution. But as years went by, the conservative trench-coat specialists got stuck in a bit of a trench themselves—styling was static and staid, and the company became relegated to the realm of honored but aging brands. It was said that Burberry lacked "profile" and exclusivity, and appealed to sedate gentlemen but not to female customers or younger ones.

Into the trenches came Rose Marie Bravo, an American with strong retail experience who took over the responsibility of rejuvenating the brand and restructuring the Burberry label for the twenty-first century. The process was not easy since the one item the company was based upon had aged: Their paradoxical mission was to make sure they made changes while

keeping things at Burberry the same.

Bravo renegotiated Burberry licenses, closed factories, and hired a dynamic new team made up of designers, an art director, and a photographer to help her create a fresh brand identity. In the best British tradition, she went back to the company's roots, unearthed its remarkable history, and began to examine it. What emerged was the "importance of the trench as the core of the brand, embodying its 'identity DNA,'" Bravo says, "and we realized that anything else we added to Burberry had to come up to the standard of the coat that stood for British luxury, sensitivity, and lifestyle. We also realized that our image was a little too skewed toward the masculine, and decided that 'feminizing' the brand, by adding women's core accessories and tinkering with the fit, would go a long way toward changing our profile."

Bravo feels that being an American in a British company was probably an asset in that it allowed her to look at Burberry free of the class-consciousness or reverence for the name that might have constrained others. She stresses the "melting pot of nationalities" that comprised her team; together, they isolated and reinvigorated the Burberry icons that made the company famous the first time around.

One of the first elements Bravo and her team seized upon was the Burberry check, resurrecting its impor-tance to the identity of the firm. They analyzed the iconic design, realizing that not only did it convey pedigree, but its neutral beige, black, and red pattern also harmonized well with almost everything. They freshened up the colors, changed the proportions, and proceeded to extend the check's use, putting the plaid on everything from neckties to flip-flops. They made it bold; they made it subtle. They cropped it. They popped it up. They milled it for a "fresco" finish, using the raw side of the fabric to give it a slightly faded look. They sometimes even tilted the tartan, manipulating the geometry to make it look different yet somehow familiar.

They then added a whole new roster of heretofore unheard-of Burberry items. In addition to the classic trench, scarves, and sweaters, they offered shirts, jeans, ties, shoes, boxer shorts, bags, and fragrances. They followed up with dresses, bandanas, caps, jeans, clothes for canines, sunglasses, and bathing suits. Bravo says when they sent the check out on the runway in its new incarnations, "it almost took on a life of its own."

When photographer Mario Testino shot model Kate Moss in a Burberry check bikini for the company's advertising campaign, it rocked the fashion world and became the symbol of the brave new Bravo-led revolution. As one writer remarked: "Until then, everyone had associated the Burberry check pattern with a coat lining to keep

Left: Kate Moss in Burberry's iconic checked bikini caused a "sea change" in the world's perception of the traditional trench coat maker. The shot is part of their brilliant black-and-white advertising campaign, photographed by Mario Testino.

you warm. All of a sudden it made its appearance on hot days—and looked cool. Burberry had managed to abstract its calling-card pattern from the purely functional."[30]

In the ensuing era of logo mania, consumers—men and women alike—could not get enough of the Burberry check: Even the Barbie Doll could be accoutered in Burberry skirt, trench coat, scarf, and bag. And although Bravo positioned the company as a luxury brand, it was a luxury brand that almost anyone could buy into with a small purchase of a fragrance or scarf or keycase.

Bravo's bravura performance was ultimately rewarded royally: In June of 2006, H.R.H. the Prince of Wales presented her with the honorary Commander of the Most Excellent Order of the British Empire title in recognition of her services to the British fashion and retail industry.

Critical to the success of Burberry's relaunch is young British designer Christopher Bailey, whose own natural style is said to coincide with that of the house. Since 2001 Bailey has been able to draw upon what Rose Marie Bravo deemed Burberry's British sensitivity, quality, and timelessness in a unique way. Having studied at the Royal College of Art in London, he apprenticed with Donna Karan and worked with Tom Ford at Gucci before his appointment as design director of Burberry. In recognition of his tremendous creative contributions—and successes—at Burberry, *Forbes* magazine named him at the top of its list of most influential designers in 2005.

In an effort to find something new in the Burberry check, Bailey says:

Each season we manipulate and translate the check in many different ways to suit the mood and attitude of the moment. This could include recolouring, resizing, oversizing, and/or shrinking, playing with the proportion or direction of the check, weaving the check in special fabrics, or placing it on garments in unexpected ways, but often, we use the iconic Burberry check in its full original glory! [31]

Bailey continues, "What I love about tartan is that it has a beautiful heritage that involves families and biographies. And I appreciate the fact that it can look wonderful in your home as well as on your body. Plaid is totally democratic: both aristocratic and rebellious, and I love the clash between the two. All the royals wear our trench coats, and the Sex Pistols wore tartan. That clash is exactly what I try to do with the Burberry aesthetic—and that's what makes the design unique, special, and sometimes sexy and aggressive."

That clash is also well represented in Burberry's enormously effective advertising. Mario Testino's campaigns with their casual, offhand—even scruffy—elegance, communicate a brand image that appeals to many, crossing both genders and generations. As Bravo herself has said, "they [the advertisements] switch very naturally from a street scene to a house in the country, from working class people to the rock-and-roll scene and nobility."[32]

Above, from left to right: Tartan on the loom at Lochcarron; the finished product; and American designer R. Scott French's gracefully back-pleated tartan skirt from his autumn/winter 2006–7 women's collection in Weathered Fraser tartan from Lochcarron.

Opposite: Scottish actor Ewan McGregor, whose family is from a town in the same region as Lochcarron, sporting a kilt for *Vanity Fair*.

LOCHCARRON OF SCOTLAND

What is the strand that connects Vivienne Westwood to Ralph Lauren to Burberry to Jean-Paul Gaultier and to so many others? Besides their common passion for tartan, it is their uncommon tartan supplier— Lochcarron, the illustrious textile mill that quite literally is the warp and the weft of those designers' collections. Lochcarron's weavers work with Westwood, enabling her to create flamboyant designs; they supply Ralph Lauren with the fabric for his luxurious upper-class classics; they provide Burberry the stuff for Christopher Bailey's edgy modern geometrics; and they furnish Jean-Paul Gaultier with the material for everything from his envelope-pushing transgender kilts to his show-stopping tartan coats.

With a home base in the Borders region of Scotland, Lochcarron has maintained its intrinsic Scottish appeal, while moving into ferociously fashion-conscious markets.

Mark Gibson, grandson of Lochcarron's founder and marketing sales director, attributes their extraordinary success in working with designers to their flexibility: "We can offer small production runs, dye and finish to specific requirements, and tie-up coordination of knitwear fabrics and garments."

Vivienne Westwood, who certainly must be considered the most inventive of designers when it comes to working with tartan can't stop raving about the firm. Having collaborated with them on the design of a number of original tartans, she says:

Lochcarron to me is the most wonderful company in the world, really, because of the choice of wool. It's possible to weave anything at that place from traditional right through to messing about and doing more innovative things, from the most wonderful tartans to thorn-proof tweeds, and they are very versatile. They have wonderful machinery and they still do everything in a traditional way.[33]

Opposite: Designer Michael Kaye's ultrafeminine tartan with leather harness detail and a froth of cascading ruffles is woven of fine merino wool in Lochcarron's Musselbrugh tartan.

Right: The Diana, Princess of Wales Memorial tartan developed by Lochcarron. Here, in a silk ball gown, designed by Elizabeth Emmanuel (pictured left) who designed Diana's wedding gown. The gown has been exhibited all over the world.

The tartan mania that has taken hold worldwide has enabled Lochcarron to expand its base considerably. Far-flung Scots and Scot wannabes continue to claim their tartans, particularly after being inspired by movies such as *Braveheart*, *Rob Roy*, and *The Last King of Scotland*, whose leads Mel Gibson, Liam Neeson, and Forrest Whitaker, respectively, were all kilted in fabric by Lochcarron. The firm's overseas growth extends to Japan where Japanese schoolgirls wear Lochcarron tartans as part of their uniforms and a local pipe band marches proudly in the firm's tartans.

In addition to working hand-in-hand with designers, Lochcarron had the honor of being chosen to develop the Diana, Princess of Wales Memorial tartan, which has enjoyed huge popularity around the globe. Diana's ancestors pertain to the Stewart clan, so the tartan was based on the Royal Stewart pattern. Its colors were selected to reflect the personality and image of the Princess of Wales: soft blues that were among her favorite shades and a red overcheck symbolizing her numerous charitable efforts. Elizabeth Emmanuel, designer of Diana's wedding gown, subsequently created a silk ball gown in the memorial tartan for exhibition around the world.

In 2002 Lochcarron presented, on behalf of the people of Scotland, the city of New York with a memorable gift: its own New York City tartan. The blue of the tartan represents the rivers surrounding the city, the green symbolizes Central Park, and its two black lines commemorate the events of September 11, 2001. Sir Sean Connery and Mayor Michael Bloomberg donned the tartan to lead New York City's first Tartan Day parade in 2002.

ALEXANDER MCQUEEN

"What attracted me to Alexander was the way he takes ideas from the past and sabotages them with his cut to make them thoroughly new and in the context of today."[34]

—Isabella Blow, stylist

As soon as Alexander McQueen finished showing the collection he designed for his master's graduation from Central St. Martin's School of Art in 1992, stylist and fashionista Isabella Blow snapped up the entire lot. Inspired by figures of the cultural demimonde, such as Jack the Ripper and Victorian prostitutes, McQueen dressed models in superbly made but outrageous creations, sending them down the runway in shocking procession. From that macabre-but-marvelous beginning, the bad boy genius of British fashion has rapidly established a reputation premised on extraordinary creativity sharpened with refined technical prowess.

McQueen honed his techniques early on, apprenticing at the tender age of sixteen with the revered Savile Row tailors Anderson & Sheppard, before moving on to Gieves and Hawkes, another bespoke tailor. He polished his theatrical flair working for costumers Angels and Bermans and designer Romeo Giglio. One of the "fashion desperadoes" who graduated from the creatively chaotic fashion cauldron that is St. Martin's, McQueen laced his early collections with historical references, infusing them with cutting-edge ideas (his derrière-bearing bumster pants) and sometimes an "aesthetic of cruelty" that he culled from his forays into anatomy and the films of Hitchcock and Pasolini.[35]

Early on in his career, he designed a seminal collection for autumn/winter 1995, ominously titled "Highland Rape," that featured a gritty catwalk tableau of blood-stained models, semiclad in the McQueen clan tartan. Resembling victims of violence in their ripped and ravaged bodices and hems, the models staggered down the heather-strewn runway like zombies. The collection provoked outrage and heavy criticism from the press. McQueen assured his critics that the "rape" was not endured by the models, but rather was a political reference to the Jacobite Rebellion in 1745, in which the Highlanders were defeated by superior British forces. (It

was suggested, at the time, that perhaps he also was influenced by the atrocities that were being committed at the time in places like Rwanda and Bosnia.) Whereas many accused McQueen of misogyny, others looked beyond what they deemed sexual politics, finding the collection "packed with restless, rousing ideas, by far the best of the London season."[36]

McQueen's creativity weathered the criticism, and a year later he was chosen to fill the position vacated by John Galliano as head designer of Givenchy, where his bizarrely beautiful technical masterpieces were received with mixed reactions. Feeling creatively constrained at the venerable French couture house, McQueen, with the help of Gucci Group, started a new company of his own in 2000, and was finally able to unleash his ideas under his own label.

He demonstrated the "quantum leap" he had made at Givenchy, in terms of technical mastery, when he revisited the Highlands for his autumn/winter 2006 collection, which he titled "Widows of Culloden" (again referring to the Battle of 1745 wherein Jacobite troops were defeated by the Duke of Cumberland's forces). Sensitive to the troubling news of the day, the seemingly endless stories of war and disaster, he felt the need to remind himself that there is beauty in the world. The designer says of his presentation:

"I wanted to show a more poetic side to my work. It was all about melancholy and sadness, but in a cinematic kind of way. I find beauty in melancholy."[37]

Using the McQueen tartan again, he designed his collection of impeccably cut suits and sinuous black velvet dresses with a melancholic poetry instead of the rawness and violence of the first tartan collection. The bold red-and-black McQueen tartan appeared at once strong and refined, in bell-shaped dresses with black lace sleeves, beautifully fitted riding jackets with black lace jabots, and swaggering, sharply tailored tartan miniskirts. McQueen described the darkly romantic collection as "very Macbeth." The press pronounced the show a rave—not only in terms of brilliant workmanship and creativity, but also as a technically accomplished performance. To wind up his return to the Highlands, McQueen ended his show with a techno-magical hologram of the fragile Kate Moss, vaporizing into the mist.

For some people of Scottish ancestry, tartan always will be steeped in politics. "I feel a strong sense of belonging and identity in tartan, as it is a part of my heritage," McQueen says, "but my attitude toward it is somewhat anarchic." Nonetheless, Alexander McQueen was awarded a CBE (Commander of the Order of the British Empire) by H.M. Queen Elizabeth II for his contributions to English fashion, an honor he wears with great pride.

Left: British designer Sir Paul Smith who likes to note: "Humour is my default setting."

Opposite: Model Lily Cole on the catwalk in Paul Smith's double-breasted russet tartan jacket during London Fashion Week autumn/winter 2005–6.

PAUL SMITH

"Paul Smith has remained for me the most interesting of designers. Because he continues to articulate something as complex as an entire culture in the remarkably restricted, yet endlessly recombinant code of fabric, texture, color, and cut."[38] —William Gibson

Paul Smith is the personification of the term "true Brit." There is an unmistakable Englishness about him—a style, a wit, a resourcefulness, and a sense of irony that seems to emanate only from the cradle of the British Empire. But now it is Smith who has built his own impressive empire on his refined, whimsical taste: His traditional, yet subtly subversive—and quintessentially British—clothes and accessories for men and women are sold in more than 250 stores around the globe, generating revenues that reach the stratosphere. The contributions to English culture and economy made by this free-spirited, eccentric, and astute businessman from Nottingham earned him the title of knight, an honor bestowed by H.M. Queen Elizabeth II.

Not bad for a guy whose ambition of becoming a professional bicycle racer was derailed by an early road accident. After Smith recovered, his mischievously restless mind turned from cycling to the world of creative arts and, having met a talented young designer and recent graduate of the Royal College of Art, Pauline Denyers, he decided to try his hand at fashion. Taking tailoring classes at night, Smith opened his first tiny shop in Nottingham, his hometown, in 1970, and with Denyers (his longtime partner and now wife) designed and sewed menswear, sowing the seedlings of the Paul Smith brand.

Smith explains that he started out as a retailer and, because he was unable to source what he wanted to sell, became a designer. During the 1970s, the emphasis was on creating individualist clothes; in Smith's words, "clothes which had character, which made you look different from everyone else." His cardinal rule was simplicity. Smith wanted his clothing to be well made, easy to wear, of good quality, and in interesting fabrics. The simple designs allowed color to become his distinctive trademark. Customers ranging from architects to corporate nonconformists found his rich colors and eccentric patterns refreshing—Smith's concept was a godsend and a huge success.

The designer allows as how his early fascination with cycling probably was the springboard for his later preoccupation with detail. As is true of most sports

enthusiasts, cyclists like Smith were obsessive about their gear—the saddles customized with hammered brass rivets, the pocketless silky rayon racing shirts, the cycling shoes with drilled soles, the white kid racing gloves, and the perfect red leather track helmets. In retrospect, he supposes this was the ideal preparation for working with fashionable iconoclasts who would devote years to finding the right shade of beige raincoat.

While Smith may have an almost genetic affinity for homegrown British fabrics, he unashamedly admits that the decision to use tweeds and tartans in early collections was one based in economic necessity: He was short on money and unable to commit to large amounts of fabric. Tartan was indigenous and available in limited yardages, so he seized upon it. To the irreverent Smith, tartan's longstanding respectability made it the perfect fabric to subvert. He took the plaids in a new direction, causing a sensation with his men's tartan anorak that featured a hood and fishtail bottom. He persuaded his Scottish mills to weave weightier versions of the fabric, and turned them into duffels and Epsom coats. With the gimlet eye of a true retailer, he bought up scores of skinny tartan schoolboy ties from Lochcarron, the Scottish weavers, and started a trend for colorful narrow ties.

The designer says that he had always loved the Scottish notion of tartan as a badge of belonging and exclusivity, rather like a family crest. Smith recalls visiting Paris, where he was struck by the sight of girls in their private-school uniforms, wheeling around Trocadero on their Solex motorbikes, in cashmere, tartan trews, and tons of self-assurance. Tartan clearly has a classiness, but an underlying sexiness besides.

Smith has found ways to incorporate tartan regularly, and often playfully, throughout his collections. The plaid is sprinkled among his men's jackets and shirts, women's skirts and pants, and especially the accessories, where checks appear on everything from proper plaid-rimmed china to clever tartan cufflinks to leather wallets and bags printed with the Black Watch pattern. Another of his favorite color/pattern plays is stripes: the Paul Smith multistriped logo shows up on many of his clothes and accessories, including the multistriped wrapping tissue and shopping bags in which you cart home your purchases.

Smith ascribes his stupendous success to an insatiable curiosity. An incurable collector of objects—ranging from kitschy to elegant varieties—he harbors a special fondness for tin robots, Bakelite radios, and rubber chickens. Each Paul Smith shop brims with his enchanting finds—jewelry, books, art, antiques,

Left: Marc Jacobs, designer of Louis Vuitton and his own eponymous collections of clothes and accessories.
Opposite: When Lily Cole led off the Marc Jacobs for Louis Vuitton autumn/winter 2004 catwalk show in Paris with her fitch-trimmed tartan coat, the audience knew they were in for something special.
Following pages: Images from Marc Jacobs for Louis Vuitton autumn/winter 2004 collection from the Paris catwalk show. Photos by Giovanni Giannoni/*WWD*/© Condé Nast Publications.

vintage toys, curios—all for sale, along with his own colorful accessories. The Paul Smith shops reflect the designer's idiosyncratic approach not only to fashion but to the entire world around him. Influenced by everything from graffiti to the tiles of the Alhambra Palace, the designer penned a book entitled *You Can Find Inspiration in Everything*. He most definitely has.

MARC JACOBS FOR LOUIS VUITTON

Marc Jacobs, the quintessential hip New York designer who is also the prodigious talent behind women's fashion and accessories for Louis Vuitton in Paris, has a modern take on tartan: "I like plaid as a design. Period. It's a bold, graphic pattern—and a perfect way to get lots of colors together." But then he adds, softly: "I like the familiarity of it, too: It makes you comfortable to see patterns that you know."

Jacobs certainly knows plaids: Some of his best collections as designer for Perry Ellis in the late 1980s and 1990s earned press plaudits for his fabulous plaids. Instead of harkening to tartan's distant historical past, though, Jacobs views plaid in the contemporary context of the music scene—how the punks wore it: tight and ripped and irreverent; how the grunge bands lived in it: loose, layered, low-key; and how street kids put it together.

Jacobs appreciates the paradoxical nature of tartan. When contemplating his autumn/winter 2004 collection for Louis Vuitton in Paris, for example, he explained that "we were coming off a very opulent season, and wanted to tone things down ... to convey luxury in a quieter way without using elaborate fabrics like brocades. Tartan, a simple fabric but with its own inherent richness—both in history and color—seemed to be the perfect choice."

The Vuitton collection was a huge hit, and Jacobs was roundly praised for making tartan and tweed look young and sexy with his body-conscious, bias-cut silhouettes. For that collection, Jacobs—who admits he's always found a romantic element in tartan—played it to the hilt with a wintry, snow-dusted runway. His plaid-clad models were a vision of white skin and red lips, wearing pearls and white fur, and toting red velvet bags.

The show also featured bits of Highland swagger

and a lot of feminine touches: leg-of-mutton sleeved blouses tucked into narrow skirts with flirty hems, lace-trimmed décolleté, bustiers, shrugs, fur tippets with satin bows, and a glamorous fitch-trimmed tartan coat. Jacobs reports that some of the collection's prettiness was inspired by the paintings of Jacques Tissot, and his collaborative staff did research in Scotland, but he himself preferred not to go. "I don't like to rely on referential material too heavily," he says, "it allows me more room for creativity."

Instead, he always has a girl in mind as his muse: Sometimes it's alternative rock drummer Meg White of the White Stripes or actress Winona Ryder. In the case of the autumn/winter 2004 Vuitton collection, it was a friend: "She's French, extroverted, and flirtatious—this tartan collection was for someone very contemporary, very real."

ISAAC MIZRAHI

"Tartan is a symbol of pride, of family. It's not at all gaudy. It has presence without being bejeweled or overdressed."

—Isaac Mizrahi

Fashion designer/actor/television personality Isaac Mizrahi maintains that he has no Celtic ancestors, insisting that if you unearth his Brooklyn roots, you won't find a Scot in the lot. Yet he is possessed by tartan mania, a passion that he skillfully wove into his early collections and continues to draw upon for designs for the mass-market chain Target and his couture collections for high-end retailers such as Bergdorf Goodman.

Mizrahi says his madness for tartan was ignited by films like Roman Polanski's *Macbeth* and stylish old romances like *I Know Where I'm Going!* Although his respect for the plaid as a symbol of Scottish pride is profound, he does not feel bound to treat tartan reverentially, preferring instead to deconstruct the classic and recontextualize it. He understands the implicit sexiness of tartan as well: Having had kilts made to order for him at Kinloch Anderson, in Edinburgh, Mizrahi is comfortable wearing them and definite that, in his view, "a kilt is not a kilt if you are wearing underwear."

He cites the dichotomy between the "the wild, crazy soulful Highlands and the genteel civilization we associate with the British Isles" as integral to tartan's appeal. The imaginative designer's blockbuster

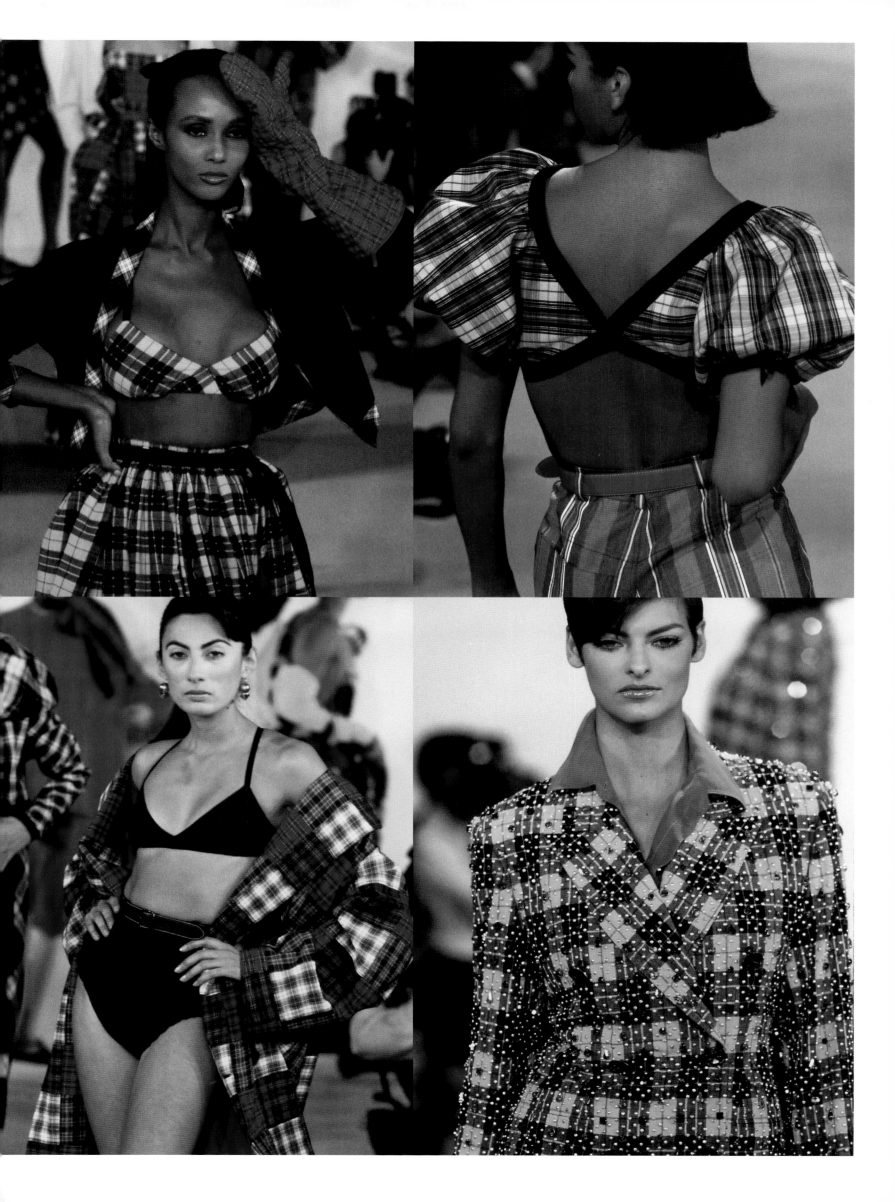

Page 180: From Mizrahi's 1991 men's collection, an oversized cashmere tartan shirt over a paisley shirt.
Page 181: Hieing off to the Highlands, Linda Evangelista in Isaac Mizrahi's flaring Royal Stewart skirt, black blazer, and beret. Arthur Elgort/*Vogue*/ © Condé Nast Publications.
Previous left page: Isaac Mizrahi's mini-McLeod patterned jacket over larger scale McLeod bikini top and minikilt.
Previous right page, clockwise from upper left: More madras Mizrahi from spring/summer 1990— Iman in a tartan halter and full skirt; cross banded puff-sleeved halter top with striped tapered pants; McLeod blazer in yellow and black; and a patchwork tartan beach cover-up.
Opposite: Linda Evangelista in Isaac Mizrahi's strapless black tulle dress, with tartan shawl and tartan hose. Photograph by Arthur Elgort/ *Vogue*/© Condé Nast Publications.

fall/winter 1989 collection, which was dominated by tartan, raised his status from up-and-coming designer to fashion supernova. The fashion press raved, calling it a "winning show" and referring to Mizrahi as Seventh Avenue's "best boy."

Mizrahi took tartan out of the realm of classic and traditional and used it in ways it had never before been, rendering it in fabrics no clansman could have anticipated—cashmere flannel, rep silk, and chiffon. He mixed his tartan colors and patterns with wit and humor. They were deemed a forerunner of a new casual attitude toward dressing—one which embodied a respect for the past and a certain irreverence in applying it to the future. The standouts in the collection were the clan tartans: a Royal Stewart strapless cashmere side-buckled kilt dress worn under a black-and-white checked silk hooded blouson and a fur-trimmed parka and a Black Watch patterned chiffon dressing gown and pajama for evening—fabrics which certainly took it beyond the traditional. If tartan has long been comforting, the designer made it comfortable as well. His shapes—sexy bathrobes, off-the-shoulder blouses, strapless kilt dresses, hooded parkas, and full, paper bag pants—turned tartan into an eased-up modern tour de force. The fashion press

raved that it was "unique" and "imaginative" and dubbed Mizrahi "The King of Tartan." Journalist Suzy Menkes got it just right when she commented that "[h]is achievement was to link upscale luxury with lively, downtown sportswear."[39]

Mizrahi continued to play up plaids in his subsequent collection for spring 1990, using madras as a background for his tartans. Instead of going the traditional preppy route, though, he ritzed-up casual cotton with brass studs and glittery jewels, giving colorful classics like the MacLeod, Gordon, and Stewart tartans a glamorous evening cachet. To the designer, "the colorful classic tartans, the MacLeod, the Gordon, and especially the Stewarts are as versatile as bold solids. I believe you can wear tartan plaids with everything."

Because Mizrahi is famous for his theatrical flair (before he studied design at Parsons, he attended New York's High School of the Performing Arts) and as he is known for his riffs on tartan, he has been commissioned often to create costumes for both dance and theater. Outstanding among them are his tartan costumes for Twyla Tharp's *Brief Fling*, which premiered at the American Ballet Theatre in 1990. For this very Scottish dance, he paired a tartan-patterned tulle tutu with a velvet bodice, a cashmere kilt and knickers, a

tartan taffeta blouson with a bodysuit, and tights with a pleated plaid satin cummerbund.

Mizrahi's latest maxim is to bring "class to the masses" via his affordably priced collections for Target. Often, among the household objects or cheap-but-chic skirts, sweaters, and tops, something tartan turns up. No matter what he says, there's a spot of Scot in Mizrahi.

MICHAEL KAYE

Growing up in Alberta, Canada, Michael Kaye saw plenty of plaid. The legacy of its original Scottish settlers, a tartan culture is woven into the country's daily life, and in Edmonton, Kaye's hometown, it is evident everywhere from the Whyte Avenue shops to the local Highland Golf and Country Club. Even the flags that represent each of Canada's provinces and territories are made of tartan.

It was those flags that really stirred Kaye's imagination. On a school trip to the Legislative building, he saw the standards of all the provinces displayed together and was indelibly impressed by the beauty, variety, and emotional impact of tartan.

A child of Ukrainian descent, Kaye was not "to the tartan born," but was determined to make the plaid part of his life. After graduating from the University of Alberta, Kaye studied at New York's Fashion Institute of Technology where he developed a sure-handed, sophisticated style. But he laughingly admits that any time he had the opportunity to inject tartan into anything he was designing, he did: "no matter what the collection was, I was always ready to push the plaid."

After designing at dress firms from Adele Simpson to Arnold Scaasi, Kaye opened his own couture business where, among other areas of expertise, he has created a specialty of tartan design. He has a particular bias for cutting tartan on the diagonal, which not only changes the geometry of the plaid, but allows him to create hand-fringed edges and circular hems to give a gown a slightly rough-hewn look.

Kaye's tartan dresses have been received with enormous enthusiasm: One of his back-pleated, bias-cut, tartan ball gowns was selected by Harold Koda for inclusion in the Metropolitan Museum of Art Costume Institute's permanent collection. In 2004 Kaye was the recipient of the Fashion Group International's prestigious "Women's Apparel" award for his innovation, creativity, and accomplishments.

Kaye has given the gift of tartan back to his home country: With the weaver Lochcarron, he helped design a tartan flag for the new Canadian territory

Nunavut. The designer has also gifted his hometown with one of his graceful gowns, done—of course—in the tartan of Alberta's flag.

PLAID PANOPLY

Scores of leading international fashion designers, especially those who are known for their bravura use of color have worked magic with tartan over the years. Some have been dedicated to the plaid aesthetic, using it on a perennial basis; others have flirted with it for a season here and there. Whatever the nationality, the panoply of plaid designers here share an appreciation for the exuberant international symbol of dignity and style, whether worn in the classic style or twisted and manipulated into a whole other mode.

Yves St. Laurent is one of the all-time masters of tartan. During his over forty years designing women's and men's fashion, he sent a plethora of plaids down the catwalk, both in his couture and ready-to-wear collections. Always a classicist, St. Laurent tailored his tartans with precision, but it was his artistry with color that made them truly remarkable. Known for borrowing ideas from menswear and tailoring them to women, he could take the elements of a man's traditional Highland military uniform from "bonnet" to "ghillies" and using beautifully hued combinations

Below: Yves St. Laurent's wool crepe tartan dress with fringed panel, under a checked, silk-lined coat from his autumn/winter 1991 collection.
Opposite: Yves St. Laurent planting a kiss on the hand of one of his models at the finale of his autumn/winter 1991 Paris catwalk show.

of velvet and cashmere and silk tartan, turn them into something quintessentially feminine, French, and modern.

Jeffrey Banks, American menswear designer and coauthor of this book, has had an obsession with tartan since he can remember. His clean-lined sportswear and dress classics for men are designed with a nod to both British tradition and American preppiness often with an unexpected twist of color. He loves toying with the geometry of tartan, playing diagonal argyle patterns against classic tartan grids.

Jean-Paul Gaultier, the multitalented and often outrageous French designer of both prêt-a-porter and couture, who is perhaps best known for dressing Madonna in a bustier, thus launching a bold, new sexiness in the way contemporary women dress, is also a tartan aficionado and a great proponent of the concept that men should have the option to wear skirts. While his women's ready-to-wear has often featured tartans, he earned enormous plaudits for the plaid coats he showed in his autumn 2007 collection in bravura tartans like the black-and-yellow Macleod, which swaggered down the catwalk, collared and bordered with fox and worn with towering matching Macleod tartan shoes.

It has often been said that tartan is a perennial, reappearing with regularity year after year, but always capable of looking new. Part of the reason for that seems to emanate from the intrinsic geometry of tartan, which is able to be manipulated in a vast number of ways; but, in the end, the real answer to tartan's ongoing appeal is more than likely in ourselves—and the infiniteness of our imaginations.

Following pages: Three classic images from St. Laurent's famous "Highland Spirit" collection show in Paris in 1991 illustrate the master's bravura use of color and texture.

Pages 196–97: Menswear designer Jeffrey Banks's country tweeds and tartan from his fall 1983 collection. Hoyt Richards in a handwoven Scottish tweed oversized sports jacket with wool challis tartan shirt and wool trousers, and Renauld White in parquet patterned tweed balmacaan, tweed Glen plaid jacket and miniature tartan shirt with cashmere scarf.

Page 198: Linda Evangelista tartan riding jacket and pants by Jean- Paul Gaultier. Arthur Elgort/*Vogue*/ © Condé Nast Publications.

Page 199: Linda Evangelista in Christian LaCroix's tartan ball gown in Dress Stewart tartan, with a pleated, fan-shaped cascade down the back, black velvet embroidery, and bow.

Previous left page: Highly innovative Japanese designer Rei Kawakubo for Commes des Garcons is well known for her deconstructed fashion as exemplified in this ensemble from autumn/winter 2000. Photo by Giovanni Giannoni/ *WWD/* © Condé Nast Publications.

Previous right page: Balenciaga on the bias— Nicolas Ghesquière's homage to the master's classic form with a stand-up collared, curved tartan suit, and mini bell skirt from autumn/winter 2006–7.

Right: Jean-Paul Gaultier, know for his gender-bending fashion, is a great proponent of skirts for men. Here the designer is in his signature look: striped Breton shirt, tartan kilt, and biker boots.

Below: Jean-Paul Gaultier's over-the-top tartan trench coats in bold plaids often lavished with fur, and worn with matching strappy tartan shoes from autumn/winter 2007.

Below: Gaultier's plaid and plumes—His corset-detailed coat done in different sized black-and-yellow McLeod tartan from autumn/winter 2007.

LIVING

"The tartan is arguably one of Western culture's most powerful patterns: you can clothe, decorate, even plan cities with its seductive geometry."

—Jaquelin T. Robertson, architect, Cooper Robertson & Partners

"Living" is an all-encompassing word, but one of its primary definitions is "dwelling." And the way we dwell is meant to speak volumes about us. "How we decorate our homes corresponds to social class, values, sex roles, and stage of life as much as it does to personal preferences. Certain styles become the rallying flags of group membership."[1] Inasmuch as tartan already has an implicit sense of "belonging," it is fascinating to see how it works in tandem with interior design, not only imparting beauty and vivid color, but also subliminally reinforcing the ideas of identity and membership in the club.

Opposite: Tartan Americana—red, white, and blue tartan in a Greenwich Village, New York City, townhouse filled with American folk art and antiques, including the rare handpainted fireman's parade hats mounted on the wall. The rooms and the tartan were designed by interior designers Diamond and Baratta.

Left: Glen Feshie Lodge—the ancestral home of the Dukes of Bedford had been reduced to half its original size when Ward Denton and Christopher Gardner were hired to renovate it. Built of local granite and timber, the castle acquired a turret and entrance hall in the process of its two-and-a-half-year restoration.
Right: H.M. Queen Elizabeth II walking cross-country on the grounds of Balmoral.

"Living" also means "living or acting out one's fantasies." A spectacular illustration of this takes place in the performance of the New York City Ballet's *Union Jack*, based in part on "the Scottish tattoo"—the traditional presentation of the clans in their full regalia. The dance won acclaim for its choreographed weaving of geometric patterns, its gorgeous exuberance, and its swirling tartan uniforms, which are only slightly modified from the military model. New York City Ballet Mistress Karin von Aroldingen, who in 1976 created the role of the commanding chief of a female marching band, described her transformative experience with tartan to Tobi Tobias in an interview for the *New York Times:* "As you put on your costume, it gave you a feeling of aristocratic elegance and respect for order. It helped you acknowledge being part of a tribe and loving the place you belong to."

In a similar vein, living or acting out one's fantasies could include everything from thousands of men kitted out in kilts piping up Sixth Avenue in Manhattan in the Tartan Day parade as if heading off to battle. Or a European businessman living the "luxe laird life" as the owner of a Scottish baronial, tartan-bedecked castle. On a lesser level, ordinary guys who just want to look like they're masters of the manor can don Ralph Lauren's gentrified plaids to channel a clan ancestry. Even in miniature scale, such as Tiffany's delightful Christmas windows, tartan can telegraph tradition, decorum, and taste.

Of the people who live truly well, we would have to consider the British royal family near the top of the list. For many of the "royals," their off-duty lives for the last 160 years have meant hieing off to the country where they *live* in tartans and tweeds. For royalty of another stripe—entertainers—tartan has a flamboyant appeal, allowing artistic expression and performing brilliantly on stage. Through its many incarnations and over time, tartan is unquestionably a *living* phenomenon.

Previous left page: Denton and Gardner covered the guest bath with a tartan wallcovering, then hung a dozen framed tartans to great graphic effect.

Previous right page: Master bedroom with bay window overlooking the roaring Feshie River. The designers softened the tartan bed curtains by adding velvet, florals, and Persian carpets. The Norwegian reindeer rack is a nod to the client's wife.

Opposite: Denton and Gardner–designed scroll-back chairs are covered in a tartan from Ralph Lauren Home Collection, which reflects the soft colors of the mural behind, depicting scenes from the estate.

GLEN FESHIE: THE QUEEN'S NEXT-DOOR NEIGHBOR

In the 2006 movie *The Queen*, featuring Helen Mirren as the besieged British monarch coping with the cataclysmic aftermath of the death of her ex-daughter-in-law Princess Diana, a lot of action takes place at Balmoral Castle. Nestled among the lochs and valleys of the Scottish Highlands, the baronial castle was the favored refuge of Queen Victoria and to this day is much beloved by the British royal family. Although the property used in the movie somewhat resembles Balmoral, some filming took place instead on the grounds of Glen Feshie Lodge, Balmoral's next-door neighbor and another grand, turreted stone-and-timber pile with its own 42,000 acres of property.

In the late 1990s, Glen Feshie was purchased by a Danish businessman who called upon the design team of Ward Denton and Christopher Gardner to decorate and reconstruct the castle and several guest-house cottages from top to bottom. Not an easy task as, like many of Britain's stately homes, it had been partially demolished when the cost of maintenance became excessive. The original building was virtually gone and the footprint had disappeared. So the team was called

upon to supply everything from the requisite nineteenth-century romanticism to the writing paper, porcelain, and coat hangers.[2] The 20,000 square-foot house, which took two and a half years to complete, required the designers to temporarily establish quarters in London in order to be close to the site and their design sources.

The new owner had admired Denton's work in his role as creative director at Polo Ralph Lauren, and the designers immediately understood that the "laird of the manor" décor requested by their client would entail tons of tartan—after all, it *was* Queen Victoria, their client's proverbial neighbor, who helped popularize the plaid. But, rather than opt for an over-the-top "MacCastle" effect, the decorators decided to go "tartan lite," using subtle, often muted versions of the plaid in almost every room, but employing it somewhat sparingly to accent other important elements. The rooms are a perfect example of how the plaid can work with tweeds, leathers, chintzes, and Oriental rugs—its bands of color visually unify a room and give depth to the other fabrics and colors in the space. In only one room do the designers deviate from their "touches-of-tartan-only" approach: a handsome powder room which layers a dozen framed tartan setts on top of tartan-patterned paper.

Below: A sleek hound head sporting an antique tartan bonnet and shawl, referencing the local preoccupation with the hunt.

Opposite: The master bedroom with an Edwardian armchair in soft, antique tartans beside a slate mantel over which is hung *Woman in White Dress*, a nineteenth-century painting. On the left is a copy of Edwin Landseer's *Monarch of the Glen*, the original of which was said to have been painted on the estate.

In selecting the tartans themselves, the designers chose many nineteenth-century shawls that might well have been woven in local districts. The tartans often are used casually, tossed over the back of a sofa or appearing on large, cushy pillows, frequently mixed with tweeds, velvets, and paisleys. The owner largely left the design team to their own devices when developing the color scheme, but he did request that his dining room chairs be done up in an exuberant scarlet tartan that, in the best "coals to Newcastle" way, it was: Denton and Gardner selected a tartan that came from an American resource—Ralph Lauren's Home Collection.[3]

Denton and Gardener hung lush tartan draperies on some of the major windows, and for the master bedroom they installed an impressive Jacobean-style bed-cum-bed-curtain. (In northern Scotland, bed curtains are enormously practical: Not only do they keep out the chill, but in summer, when the sun almost never sets, they keep out the light.) The decorating team mixed wonderful Scottish and English hunting paintings and a number of fishing motifs with the tartans, and it all works in casual but splendid harmony. In fact, one of the paintings in the master bedroom, a copy of Edwin Landseer's 1850 work, *The Monarch of the Glen*, is said to have been painted on the estate. Unsurprisingly, the magnificent stag that is depicted looks very much like the noble beast the Queen encounters in the eponymous movie.

Below left: The dining room from another perspective. Guest chairs are upholstered in a muted green, blue, and black tartan but the host's chairs are in bright red McPherson tartan.

Below right: The drawing room's muted browns, greens, burgundies, and butterscotch, punched up by vivid tartans and paisleys. By evening firelight, the pale linen walls give a lightness to the room.

Following pages: Jeffrey Banks's personal collection of tartanware, representing the utilitarian items deemed necessary to Victorian life—napkin rings, snuff boxes, threadboxes, boxes for needles, pins, cigars, letters, and tea caddies—all in a plethora of different plaids.

TARTANWARE

"When I bought my first piece of tartanware, I knew I had to have more. There is something completely attractive and addictive about all those plaids."

—Jeffrey Banks

In the mid-nineteenth century, when Queen Victoria and Prince Albert chose Balmoral as their preferred royal residence, the popularity of Scotland—particularly the romanticized Highlands—began to swell and tourists discovered a new destination. The ensuing frenzy for all things Scottish, waggishly referred to it as "Balmorality," flourished famously during the latter half of the nineteenth century.

In order to feed the tartan mania, manufacturers invented not only new tartans but new tartan objects, and among the most appealing were a series of household goods called tartanware. With their penchant for practicality, the Victorians turned out tartan-patterned items to use in every facet of their quotidian lives— snuffboxes, letter openers, tea caddies, needle cases, hourglasses, egg cups, piggy banks, and parasol handles, to mention just a few. When tourists left the Highlands, their bags were brimming with these charming souvenirs of Scotland, which then made their way around the world. Scottish businesses also sent them out as a gift to customers with an order, further assuring their wider circulation within the country.

At first, the tartan patterns were drawn by hand on wood (mostly sycamore), a painstaking and costly process. W. and A. Smith of Mauchline, in Ayrshire, Scotland, two brothers who had one of the bigger snuffbox manufacturing businesses, saw their business decline when Queen Victoria decreed snuff-taking vulgar and common. Anticipating the need to diversify and produce a less costly product, they invented an ingenious ruling machine that allowed them to ink

tartans on paper, after which the paper was glued to the wooden objects. Paper joints were masked by black paint and embellished with gold lines. The most common patterns used were Stewart, McDonald, McGregor, McDuff, MacBeth, and Prince Charlie. Often the name of the clan tartan represented was written in tiny gold letters on the side, sometimes eccentrically misspelled. A series of lacquer coatings (copal varnish, an amberlike resin) was applied to create a patina for the plaid. The finished product was a handsome and hardy object, many of which survive and thrive into the twenty-first century.

RALPH LAUREN HOME

Tartan is said to be more a way of life than a fabric. The designer, who has applied the plaid to almost every surface imaginable, muses about why he might be able to take liberties with the fabric where others don't. He explains:

> *I think I have more freedom to work in novel ways with tartan because I am not Scottish or English. For me, there are no rules or restrictions when it comes to colors or scale of patterns or what works with what. I like the ability to take something like tartan and expand upon it—using its discipline, but framing it in entirely different ways. That, for example, is what led me to design tartan furniture: adopting an idea, adapting it to a new form, giving it a new scale and proportion. I was inspired by nineteenth-century tartanware boxes which I've always collected, and in addition, by the mostly tartan collection of clothing I had done [in fall 1991]. All of which brought me to: "why not look at tartan in a new way?" And I decided to try to apply tartan patterns to furniture for our home collection.*

Unlike his antique boxes, which are covered in tartan paper, his furniture demanded a more durable surface. Working with Frederick Edward, a furniture manufacturer in High Point, North Carolina, Lauren helped develop a silk-screen process that provides a plaid surface to new mahogany furniture. First, the tartan design is printed on paper with silk-screen inks, and the paper is soaked in water. The pattern then becomes a sheer film, capable of bonding to the mahogany.[4] The designer recounts proudly: "People

Opposite: Ralph Lauren Home Collection in the Madison Avenue store.

Right: Fall 1991 Ralph Lauren Home Collection with tartan desk.

Following left page: Breakfast at Tiffany's—Robert Rufino's tablesetting.

Following right page: Tiffany holiday windows 2005 by Robert Rufino—Cut-out tartan ornaments suspended from a tartan tree, piled with children's toys.

told me that the wonderful thing about the furniture was that it looked like something that had always existed. That, to me, was the best kind of compliment."

So it has been with Lauren's approach to tartan: He works with the fabric consistently and appreciates its associations with ancient tradition but has hijacked its use in ways the Highlanders never could have imagined. In the process, he has placed tartan in the designer lexicon on a permanent basis. In the total world of Ralph Lauren, it would be possible (albeit unlikely) for a man to sit at a tartan desk in his tartan jacket, tartan sweater, tartan shirt, tartan tie, tartan trousers, and tartan boxers. His wife might wear a tartan dress with tartan shoes or, alternatively, a tartan jacket, tartan blouse, and tartan skirt. Both might have removed their tartan coats and tartan scarves and left their tartan umbrellas in the stand. They could sit down to a dinner at a table covered with tartan linens on which are placed tartan porcelain, tartan napkins, and crystal goblets etched with a tartan pattern. They might even retire to their bedroom in tartan robes, wherein they might rest on tartan bed linens and have, of course, Technicolor tartan dreams.

CHRISTMAS AT TIFFANY'S

Tiffany & Co.'s windows on the corner of Fifth Avenue and Fifty-seventh Street in Manhattan have been likened to a uniquely fabulous and accessible art gallery open 24/7 to anyone and everyone in the world. The quintet of windows marching left around the corner from Fifth to Fifty-seventh is small by most store standards, but their importance cannot be underestimated. Displaying gorgeous jewels and other glittering objects in witty, miniature juxtapositions of scale and texture, the tableaux are art, sculpture, and theater at the same time. Their intent is not merely to sell merchandise, but to reflect the tone and tenor of the store as well: They are truly windows on the soul of Tiffany.

For Robert Rufino, Tiffany's vice president of creative services, nothing is more exciting than conjuring the magic of the store's celebrated Christmas windows. The holiday season following the events of September 11, 2001, however, was particularly challenging. The mood in New York City was still very somber in November when the windows were to be installed,

and Rufino felt he needed to strike a balance. He wanted to depict the glorious festivity of the holidays but thought it should be done in an intimate and homey way. At the same time, he felt it was important to pay homage to the bravery of the city's inhabitants.

Rufino chose tartan—a pattern often associated with the holidays—as a unifying theme for the window displays. For the designer, tartan signifies a sense of belonging, a feeling of family and home. In each scene, the main characters are a family of tiny snow-people going about their Christmas rituals, all swathed in tartan scarves, piling plaid-wrapped packages in their sleigh, hanging tartan stockings by the fire, toasting the New Year with hope, all the while sporting Tiffany baubles and tartan. Rufino then added tiny American flags to each scene as a tribute to the courage and spirit of those who were involved in the terrible events.

On the November day when the Christmas windows were installed, a remarkable number of people turned out on Fifth Avenue. To the amazement of *New York Times* photographer Bill Cunningham, who was photographing the windows' unveiling, scores of women appeared dressed in tartan. There was a palpable feeling in the air that people were wrapping themselves in the tradition and security of tartan because it protected them in an uncertain world.

In the fall of 2005, Rufino returned to the tartan theme, this time in a more architectural vein. The windows mixed up the geometry of tartan, with bias-cut trees and ornaments arrayed against solid architectural forms. Rufino designed an entire fireplace mantel in a classic red-and-green tartan, then recolored it in slews of purples and blues, drawing up to the fire a couple of comfortable tartan chairs. In another window, he placed tartan busts of a man and a woman—scarved, hatted, and bejeweled—arranged behind a shimmering assortment of champagne flutes.

It has been said that "the essence of tartan is display" and Tiffany's holiday 2005 windows were a perfect three-dimensional exhibit of the showiness of the plaid in all its exuberant color, richness, and depth.

DIAMOND AND BARATTA

"We've always loved tartan: it's traditional, stylish, geometric, patterned, and cute. We use it so much, it's like a solid. We must have been Scottish in another life."[5]

—Bill Diamond

If nature abhors a vacuum, then Bill Diamond and Tony Baratta, the dynamic design duo who have never seen a bare wall they didn't want to cover, are in perfect accord. In a world of interiors dominated by minimalist neutrals, the team has carved a colorful niche for themselves with their detailed, take-it-to-the-max mode of decorating. Using bold, pattern-on-pattern schemes, pumped-up proportions, and fearless originality, Diamond and Baratta toy with tradition, transforming it into something unexpected, joyous, and one-of-a-kind. Theirs is bravura design.

For a couple of over-the-top designers, Diamond and Baratta had fairly classical educations. Diamond graduated from Carnegie Mellon University with a Bachelor of Arts in design and painting and worked for New York designer Pauline Feldman for twelve years before opening his own shop. Baratta received his B.A. in art history from Fordham University and started working as Bill's assistant the day after he graduated, eventually becoming his business partner. Both agree that art has always inspired them in their work and anyone who has seen their color-soaked rooms would quickly concur.

But another great asset they bring to the party (and decorating with them is definitely a party!) is a marvelous sense of visual humor. Once dubbed "the Nichols and May" of their profession, Diamond and Baratta devise witty riffs on familiar themes, reinventing them as they go along. But there's a method to their madness: wallcoverings are overscaled, but traditional; upholstered sofas and chairs, though Brobdingnagian in size, are classic in shape. And "the fabrics, which look as if someone ran them through the copier on the enlargement setting and then twiddled the dial for outrageous color combinations, are actually meticulously rescaled and colored by the designers and woven to order."[6]

With their emphasis on the colorful and exuberant, it seems fitting that tartan weaves its way into many Diamond and Baratta schemes. "It's a natural fabric for us," says Tony Baratta, "as we pile on florals, stripes, and checks, we always want to add tartan—it has the ability to pull a whole look together. But, of course, we juice up the tartan's coloring and scale it in different ways." The grand, two-story entrance hall of a country house they did is a case in point, featuring soaring architecture and walls covered in an ultra-magnified

form of Stewart tartan fabric, recolored in a blazing sunflower yellow tartan that's more riotous than royal. The idea, according to the designers is to bring new meaning to tartan (and other classics like houndstooth checks, argyles, and tweeds) by weaving them in bold colors and proportions, thus transforming the familiar and classic into something akin to Pop art.[7]

The designers are truly dyed-in-the-wool tartan fans. Diamond gleefully confesses that when he was in high school, he tooled around in a shiny red Oldsmobile Cutlass that was outfitted with red tartan carpeting. He took weaving classes in school to learn the structure of the fabric and is frequently inspired to create his own tartans, or rework classic setts in unclassic colors. A particularly successful example is a take he did on the popular Stewart tartan: Most often seen in red, the plaid develops a distinctly different personality in pinks and blues. While the pattern remains reassuringly familiar, the colors are cool and modern, rather more Gustavian than Glaswegian.

For years Diamond and Baratta had contented themselves with Lee-Jofa's fine traditional Scottish tartans, but one day, they approached the company with the idea of producing their own supersized, supercolored line on, of course, supergigantic looms. After production had started and when the weavers realized the scope of what they were creating, they stopped the looms and gathered around, stunned. The color and bravado of the tartan setts looked as though they could only have been woven by hand—an enormous hand. The weavers burst into spontaneous applause for themselves—and for the daring designers who came up with the outsized idea.

Diamond and Baratta acknowledge that a great many of their show-stopping pieces depend on custom work and to this end they have gathered a guildhall of crackerjack craftsmen and artisans. They are known for taxing the limits of the textile printers and weavers with whom they work in their quest for over-the-top proportions. One Vermont weaver was forced to rent an entire gymnasium to complete a sixty-foot oval-braided rug that was destined for a great hall in one of their client's country homes.

Although Diamond has confessed that he likes to devise a new tartan for every client, he also might play off an existing plaid. In a playful den, he repeatedly layered the renowned Buchanan tartan in its striking greens, oranges, and yellows. As Gregory Cerio writing for *House and Garden* described, "The pattern was enlarged for upholstery and again for a startling tartan rug, woven like a fabric from tight, finger-thick wool yarn. It's as if a kilt for a giant has been laid on the floor."[8]

Left: Designers Diamond and Baratta use the greens, oranges, and yellows of Buchanan tartan in varying proportions to create a den with warmth, texture, and eye-popping pattern.

In the introduction to their recent book *Diamond Baratta Design,* which features the last twenty-five years of their extraordinary work, the design team reiterates the important point that in order to design the unique and idiosyncratic residences that they do, they depend upon a great deal of custom work and the expertise of "an extensive network of craftspeople and artisans who use old-world techniques to make furnishings for today: weavers, textile printers, muralists, braiders, needlepointers, upholsterers, quilters, embroiderers, and cabinetmakers …because we do so much couture work, we can specify the exact shades we want and apply them in new ways and daring combinations …our control over color lets us layer pattern on pattern in a harmonious way."[9]

By using traditional materials in novel and imaginative ways, scaling them in new proportions, and endowing them with bold color, Bill Diamond and Tony Baratta have infused tartan—and checks, argyles, and tweeds—with a modernity, energy, and meaning for a whole new audience. And they've had a lot of fun doing it, besides.

ANTA

*"Tartans rather suit the Scottish temperament of humor
blended with seriousness. There is something slightly coquet-
tish about tartan plaid."*

—Annie Stewart, cofounder and director, ANTA

Annie and Lachlan Stewart have mastered the art of
modern tartan. The dynamic husband-and-wife team,
who met at Edinburgh College of Art, melded his
architect/restorer/furniture-maker talents with her flair
for designing innovative tartans and tweeds to create
ANTA—a textile and ceramics company situated on
the Firth of Moray on Scotland's rugged northeast
coast. Known for its quirky takes on traditional tartan
and its insistence on natural materials and fine craftsmanship, ANTA combines the best of old and new
worlds, resurrecting ancient weaving techniques and
patterns while pioneering modern concepts in design.
To top it all off—quite literally—Lachlan Stewart,
head of ANTA's architectural practice, bought and
restored a roofless, derelict sixteenth-century Z-plan
tower house known as Castle Ballone, which now
contains not only the Stewart family but also serves as
a template for living with contemporary tartan designs,

such as handcrafted fabrics and furnishings like floor-
cloths, cushions and chairs, plates and porridge bowls,
mugs and teapots.

It has not always been romance and castles for
ANTA. As newlyweds, the Stewarts lived in a light-
house with no water or electricity and rowed to work.
Annie first set out in business to create intricate tartan
patterns in silk, but because the silk yarn was costly,
she was able to produce just a few yards. With charac-
teristic resourcefulness, she worked the silk into some
knockout tartan ties and sold them to emporia like
Paul Smith boutiques and Harrod's, where they flew
out of the stores.

Their resourcefulness was tested again when they
were late to set up ANTA's exhibit for the Decorex
trade fair one season in England, and decided at the
last minute—almost as a joke—to deck the walls and
plastic ceilings of the family camper with tartan fabric,
hang a tartan canopy out front, and sell their wares
from the vehicle itself. Annie cheerily explains, "It's in
the blood—all the Scottish tinker families who live in
caravans are called either Stewart or McGhie. They say
the Stewarts are either tinkers or kings—and Lachlan's
family is most definitely tinker." [10]

While Lachlan set about the daunting task of restoring

Left: Annie and Lachlan Stewart's tartan caravan which they transformed from its usual plastic décor into a display vehicle to showcase their wares at a textile trade show. Tartan-tented ceiling, upholstery, cushions, ceramics are all by ANTA.

Castle Ballone from the ground up, Annie worked on developing the company. With their move to northeastern Scotland, ANTA grew and expanded, consolidating headquarters, factory, pottery studio, and workshops into one area. They produce everything they sell—from the clay, to the design of the shapes and colors, to the glazes that finish them. Annie says, "We are passionate about manufacturing the things we design because it keeps our vision true. It's the way we see it and not someone else's interpretation."

She has her own take on tartan, forged as both artist and weaver:

Tartan is an ordered way of introducing a riot of colour in a very restrained manner because the design in the warp is the same as the design in the weft. The true colour that is created by the crossing of the warp with the weft is strong, but easier to look at because of the grid design. It remains organic instead of psychedelic even when vivid colours are used.

From the beginning, Annie's aim was to make tartan contemporary. She often draws upon the colors of the dramatic Highlands' land and seascape visible from their cliff-top castle, such as the golds, greens, and blues of the fields. And the sea and sky also provide endless inspiration. Annie's modern take on color gives her classic tartan designs a fresh look. For example, she redesigned the color palette of the traditional Royal Stewart tartan to include olive green and purple and exclude the black, making the pattern more suitable for home furnishings. Dubbed the "Lachie Stewart" after her husband and her eldest son, the pattern has been so versatile that she's woven it in a superluxe silk version as well. Today ANTA's fashion and furnishing fabrics, cushions, and stoneware are all sold through shops in Edinburgh, Aviemore, and on Sloane Square in London, as well as in Japan and the U.S.

In line with their "keep it real" philosophy, Annie and

Lachlan made a point of trying to restore their six-teenth-century castle with historically accurate materials and techniques. They've used authentic, indigenous materials like limestone to wash the outside walls with color and new local wood that will age beautifully inside—there are no faux-medieval touches anywhere. And although there is tartan in every room, no overwhelmingly "Scottish interior" look dominates. According to Annie, "We have used all different tartans in each room. Lots of tartans work together, but there is a very fine line between kitsch and stylish. What it's really all about is colour and how you use it."

THE DORCHESTER

When internationally renowned interior designer/architect Thierry W. Despont was tapped to create a new interior for London's fabled Dorchester Hotel's Grill, he drew upon his own impressions of what "living British" means. Imbued with the romanticism of Scottish castles, the Grill is a warm and, at the same time, modern space that uses tartan to provide texture, color, and unity, while conjuring up the essence of style world travelers associate with Scotland and Great Britain.

The Despont-designed room uses tartan in a sophisticated manner, as befits the context of an international dining spot in a superb British hotel. The plaid is presented subtly and sparingly, yet has an important presence. Along the walls, a series of voluptuous, neo-Victorian banquettes are cozy and inviting in deep navy, red, and green tartan or royal red, strewn with tartan pillows. A mix of soft gray and blue tartan or burgundy, orange, and burnt umber chairs are grouped around crisp white linen-covered tables, and candlestick lamps, capped with red shades shed an intimate romantic light. Juxtaposed against the tartan rugs and furnishings in different colors and scales, are soft sienna leathers and dramatic lighting. And the pale yellow wallcoverings and gloriously proportioned windows are no doubt designed

to give the illusion of light and warmth on the gloomiest winter day.

But perhaps the most impressive elements in the grill are painter/sculptor Mark Beard's heroic and heroically proportioned ten-foot-tall murals featuring swashbuckling tartan-clad gentlemen, properly outfitted with sporrans and swords, who at first glance seem to be figures out of the nineteenth century, but, upon closer inspection, seem to possess an ironic air that is strictly of-the-moment. The multitalented Beard is well known for the idealized figures he sculpts and paints, many of which are in museums around the world. He has also created the magnificent sporting figure murals that loom several stories high in Abercrombie & Fitch's New York and London flagship stores.

RANDALL A. RIDLESS

In the late 1990s when Burberry chief executive Rose Marie Bravo tapped renowned interior designer Randall A. Ridless to redesign the company's stores in its new hip image, she was already well attuned to his remarkable conceptual creativity. Ridless had been part of Bravo's creative team before, having collaborated with her on design projects at retail powerhouses like Macy's, I. Magnin, and Saks Fifth Avenue. But what

Bravo, Ridless, and their team accomplished at Burberry was revolutionary: Not only did they reverse the company's solid but stodgy image, they forever altered the way the world would look at reinventing a brand. And one of their primary tools was tartan or, as Burberry likes to call it, "the check."

The designer's commission was to design a new retail environment for Burberry's global flagship on Bond Street in London, and then using it as a prototype, translate its character physically into different Burberry stores worldwide. Ridless devised parts and pieces that could be used interchangeably whether in a 26,000-foot freestanding store or a 5,000-square-foot duty-free shop, so that the Burberry image would always remain consistent. He says that his directive from Bravo was to design a clean, crisp space, but one that reflected warmth and British heritage, without resorting to trophies, antique luggage, or other props. As the designer recalls:

We did give a lot of attention to the notion of reinterpreting the Burberry check using the pattern in subtle ways, through a variety of colors, textures, and finishes. We developed materials that grew out of the classic camel, black, and red check: marquetry panels, tumble limestone, and antique bronze, as well as English oak and red Venetian plaster to represent the color blocks and structure of the plaid; layers of macassar ebony, blonde oak, and zebrawood alongside glass and stone to supply both glamour and modernism.[11]

The famous facades of the Burberry stores are also subtle architectural abstractions of the Burberry check, serving as "billboards for the brand," according to Lance Boge, design director for Gensler Architects, the firm responsible for the architecture of the building. The facade of the six-story New York store on Manhattan's Fifty-seventh Street is "an asymmetrical grid of caramel limestone overlaid with aluminum mesh for a fabriclike texture," which *suggests* but is *not* a check—"it is an image that telegraphs the Burberry brand."[12] Ridless adds it was Bravo's idea that in each city where there's a Burberry presence, in addition to its signature visual components, special design elements specific to each location are added to make each store unique. For example, in Japan's Tokyo Burberry, in the Omotesando district, there is a light play from the interior of the store that is used to suggest a gridlike architecture; in the Barcelona Burberry in Spain, there are checks with a Gaudíesque influence, created by stained-glass windows and mosaics, as a tribute to the city's famous architect and native son Antoni Gaudí.

In 2005 Ridless was offered the chance to put his tartan expertise to use in its country of origin: His firm was chosen by developer Wasserman Real Estate Capital to work on the renovation of the historic St. Andrews Grand, a former hotel overlooking the first tee and final hole of historic St. Andrews's Old Course, one of Scotland's most prized and venerable golf institutions. The Grand is in the process of being converted into a world-class private club with luxury residential suites. After its glory days in the early part of the twentieth century, the hotel was converted into a hospital, and ultimately a college dorm for the University of St. Andrews, whereupon it was divided into a rabbit warren of students' rooms. The extensive conversion will preserve the exterior architecture of the Victorian red sandstone building with its impressive cupola, but the interior of the building will be reconstructed from the ground up. Ridless's mission is to plan and design the interiors, not the way they were, but the way they might have been in an idealized world, creating three- and four-bedroom residences that couple fantasies of another era with every possible modern amenity. Even though the "envelope" of the building is Victorian, Ridless will install a mix of periods inside, including a number of architectural elements inspired by late eighteenth-century architect Robert Adam.

Below left: Renderings of Ridless's designs for rooms at the forthcoming St. Andrews Grand Hotel, on the edge of the fabled golf course—a yellow guest bedroom, where the tartan window treatment frames a view of the golf course, and the half-canopied tartan bed and contrasting tartan rug are played against the Gothic architectural elements.

Below right: The Great Hall with its large bay overlooking the course, uses a combination of tartans and textures and dark woods to give the space a traditional, but contemporary air.

Opposite: People who like tartan—Barbra Streisand in
New York City, shooting Vincente Minnelli's *On a Clear
Day You Can See Forever*, strolls through the park
in a tartan minicoat.

With his prodigious experience in the field, Ridless immediately turned to tartan as one of his first design elements, knowing that its classic patterns could work with both traditional and contemporary styles, evoke references to both Scotland and golf, and unify the old and the new. His plans include the use of masses of tartan in some of the large-scaled club rooms, and smaller more casual doses of the plaid in the wood-panelled living quarters, mainly in the form of accents like pillows, lampshades, occasional rugs, and throws. To further weave in the theme, the club has even created its own St. Andrews Grand tartan—in blue (inspired by the view of the sea), green (for the golf course), orange (for the exterior of the Victorian sandstone residence), white (for peace), and black (as a binder). The St. Andrews Grand is expected to open in the spring of 2008.

LIVING ROYALLY

It has been said that the British royal family has always provided the best endorsement for tartan because they actually wear it. But when Queen Elizabeth II dresses in her familiar tartans and tweeds, it's more likely a function of custom, comfort, and utility than fashion: To her—and her family for generations—tartan is a way of living, as suited to the misty, boggy countryside, as tea is to scones. And to those who admire her rusticated English country style—and wish to cultivate a bred-in-the-bone aristocratic image—tartan is a way of indicating instant "heritage."

Rock royalty—musicians and performers—employ tartan as a mode of performance art: For 1950s pioneer of rock 'n' roll Bill Haley, his country-club tartan dinner jacket likely served as a civilized "cover" for his throbbing guitar beat. For Johnny Rotten and Malcolm McLaren, their punkish plaids screamed antiestablishment; for Guns N' Roses' frontman Axl Rose, his rocker kilts provided a sexy, macho image; and for Madonna, who comes by her passion for the plaid naturally—as she is married to the Scot, Guy Ritchie—tartan kilts frequently play a role: in her "Re-Invention" tour of 2004, she and her muscle-bound male dancers all donned tank tops, kilts to the ankle, and boots to fabulous gender-bending effect.

Surprisingly, even Hollywood royalty has been living in tartan for years: from silent screen star Gloria Swanson (who wore Technicolor tartan, though it was filmed in black and white) to legends Ava Gardner, Lucille Ball, singer/actress/director Barbra Streisand, and the hilarious Peter Sellers. The plaid has played major roles in films as in Mel Gibson's epic about

Left: Karin von Aroldingen, principal dancer of the New York City Ballet, leading her troupe of troops in George Balanchine's *Union Jack*. The ballet was created to honor the British heritage of the U.S. on the occasion of its Bicentennial.

William "Braveheart" Wallace, who rallies his band of men in plaid and paint; Liam Neeson's *Rob Roy*, in which he performs his heroic deeds in the beloved fabric; the movie *Brigadoon* which captivated audiences by mixing tartan and music in the romantic mists. And on the small screen, Charlotte and Trey's memorable wedding episode on *Sex and the City*, which exhibited the joyous and celebratory side of the tartan.

American aristos, too, are into tartan, especially if they have a wee dram of Scot in them. Malcolm Forbes made a point of wearing his tartan. And his children were dressed in kilts, too, as they sailed off on their boat "The Highlander."

"Dressed to Kilt," a popular Scottish fashion extravaganza that takes place in New York City during the annual Tartan Week celebration in April (and again in Los Angeles in the fall), is an insider's look at how both traditional and contemporary tartan is worn. A roster of stars from Sean Connery to Ewan McGregor and the best-looking, bare-chested New York City firemen dress up in kilts; and a diverse group of actors, athletes, and celebrities like Jock Soto, Ann Currie, Kyle MacLachlan, Ted Turner, Eric Dickerson, Stirling Moss, and Donovan Leitch strut their tartan stuff on the catwalk to wildly appreciative audiences.

When you think about it, "tartan has been part of a living heritage which has changed to suit the needs of each new generation and which will doubtless continue to do so."[13]

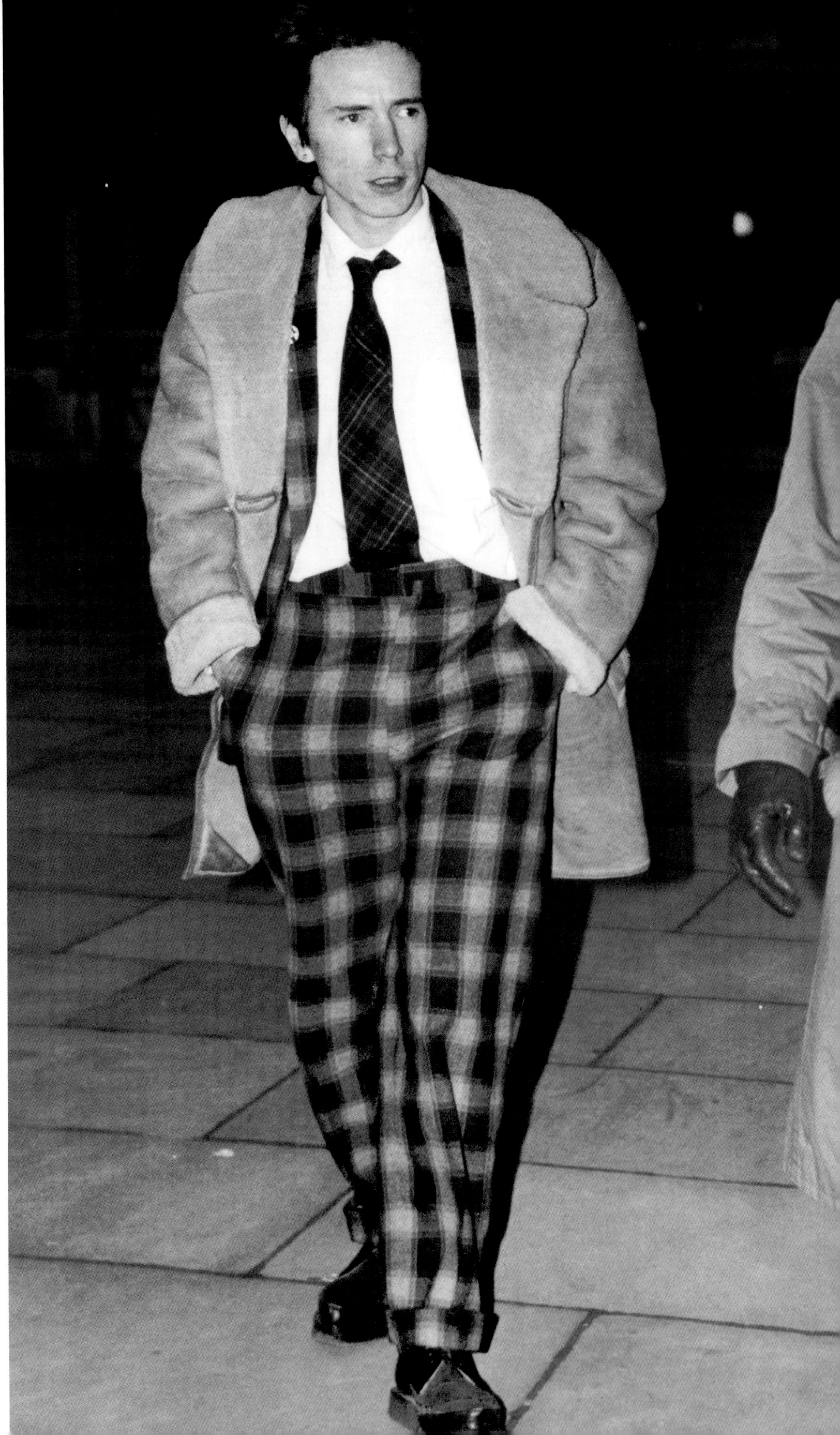

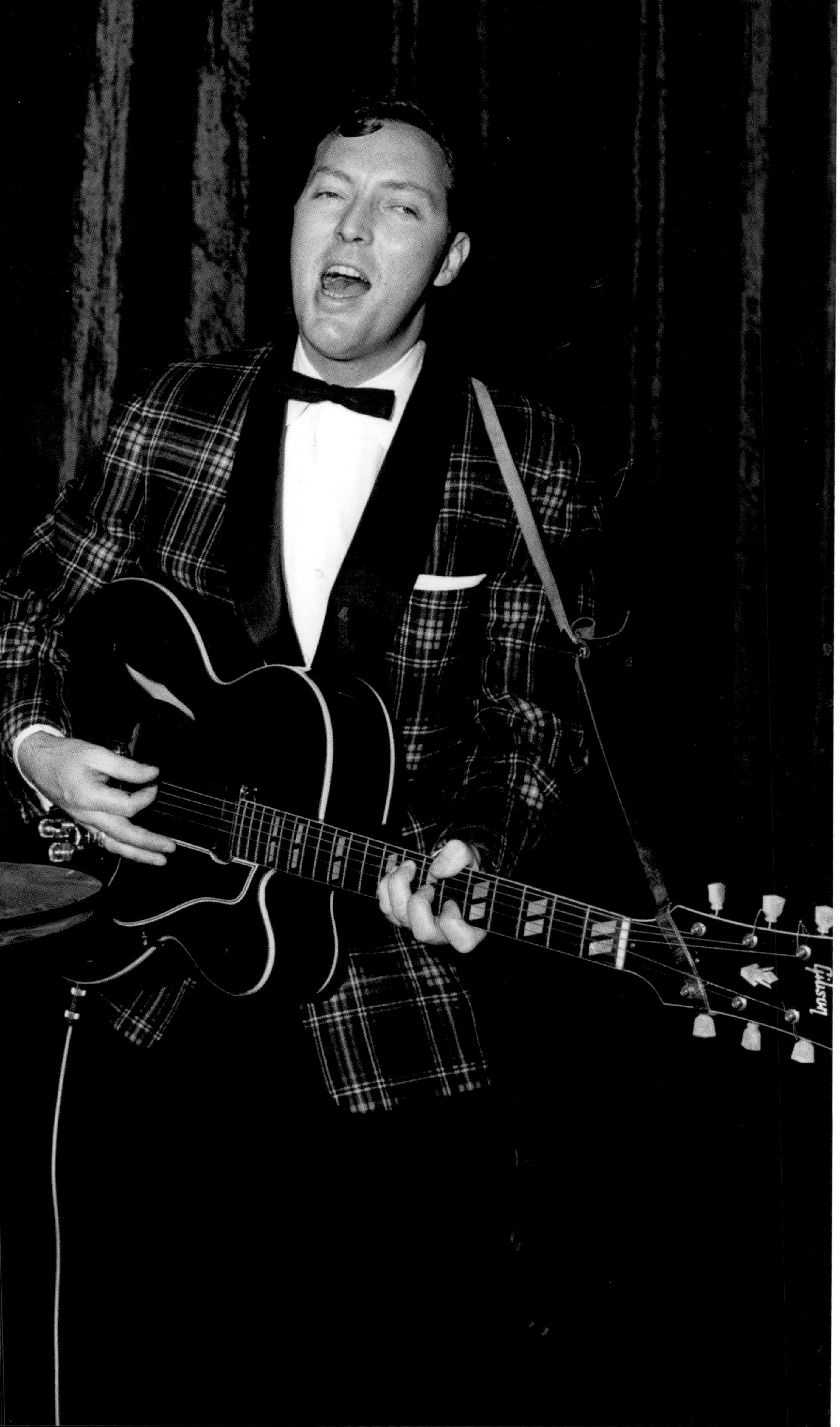
Gibson

Previous left page: Punkster John Lydon, a.k.a Johnny Rotten, former lead singer of the band The Sex Pistols.

Previous right page: Bill Haley, the American singer and guitarist, often considered the father of rock 'n' roll, at rehearsals in London.

Below left: Bay City Rollers on the set of the 1976 TV program "Shang a Lang." Formed in Edinburgh, the Scottish group got its name by randomly pointing at a map of the U.S and landing on Bay City, Michigan. Their recording, "Keep on Dancing" became a hit with dedicated fans who wore tartan in emulation of their idols.

Below right: Madonna performing in ankle length kilt and
boots during her "Re-Invention" world tour in 2004.

Below right: Madonna performing in ankle length kilt and
boots during her "Re-Invention" world tour in 2004.

Below: Gary Van Dis, Condé Nast executive, working the catwalk in the 2006 "Dressed to Kilt" show.

Opposite: Hugh Laing, the dancer and actor, performs a ballet maneuver in traditional Highland dress and ballet slippers in a publicity portrait for the film, *Brigadoon*, directed by Vincente Minnelli, 1954.

Previous pages: Liam Neeson takes aim in the film *Rob Roy*, 1995, directed by Michael Caton-Jones. Mel Gibson, raising the battle cry in *Braveheart*, 1995, which he also directed. Both films had a great impact on the resurgence of kilt and tartan-wearing among Scottish men.

Right: Model Marcus Schenkenburg appearing in the 2003 "Dressed to Kilt" show during Tartan Week in Los Angeles.

Opposite: "Dressed to Kilt" celebs on the catwalk, clockwise from upper left: Victor Webster, Ed Quinn, Eric Dickerson, and Chris Cusiter.

Following left page: Actor Sean Connery at a ceremony where he was honored with the William Wallace Award, April 5, 2001, in Washington, D.C., in celebration of National Tartan Day.

Following right page: Tartan huddle—The Scottish relay team during the 1998 Commonwealth Games in Kuala Lumpur, Malaysia.

Previous left page: Up against the wall—British punks used tartan as a form of protest against the establishment.

Previous right page: Prim plaid—Portrait of 1920s actress Claire Eames in white collared and cuffed tartan blouse with leg o' mutton sleeves. Photo by Edward Steichen /*Vanity Fair* 1925/Condé Nast Archives/Corbis.

Right: Pink Panther plaid—Actor/comedian Peter Sellers in a different kind of "cast," his leg in plaster as a result of breaking his ankle. Sellers learned another advantage to a kilt: it's easier to put on over a cast than any pants you can name.

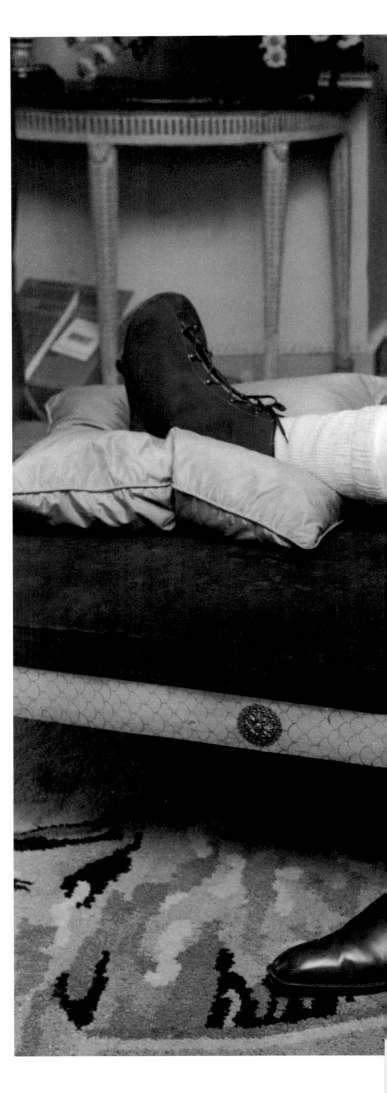

Below left: Tartan wedding belles—The bride in Michael Kaye's taffeta moiré skirt and Brodie shawl and the minibridesmaid belle is in a Brodie tartan-sashed silk dress.

Below right: The episode from *Sex and the City* where Charlotte and Trey get married, with the groom and his attendants in tartan.

Left: H.M. Queen Elizabeth II with Princess Anne, Prince Charles, and their nurse, Helen Lightbody at a stall during a Sale of Work event in Abergeldie Castle, near Balmoral. They are raising funds for the building of a new vestry at Craithie Church.

Following left page: Prince Charles in his favorite Highland garb and with Camilla, his wife (lower left).

Following right page: Princess Diana in a tartan shirtwaist dress, chatting with an unidentified bishop during a walking tour.

Below left: American Royalty—Malcolm Forbes in Scottish attire on the rooftop of his Palais Mendoub, contemplating his birthday extravaganza to which he invited celebrities from the world over.

Below right: The Forbes Five—Malcolm Forbes's children when they were mere kids in kilts, aboard "The Highlander", 1965. They are from left: Steve, Kip, Moira, Tim, and Bob.

Following pages: Having a ball with tartan—The Young Friends of the Frick Museum at a tartan ball in February 2001, where almost everyone turned up in the plaid, whether traditional, contemporary, or just plain grand.

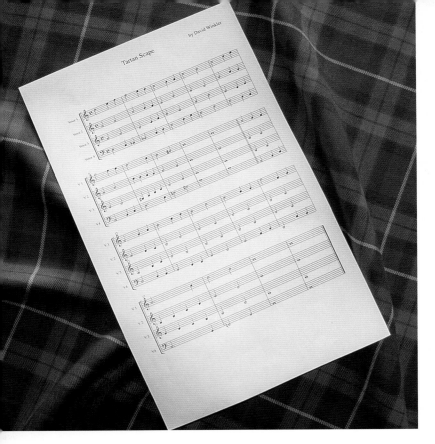

Left: Plaid to be played—It has been said that schematically, tartan can be represented as a musiclike system of motif, reverse motif, and repeat, working both horizontally and vertically. Composer David Winkler was inspired to write an original piece of music, which he calls "Tartanscape," based on the fabric's woven rhythms. © 2007 David Winkler.

Opposite, from left to right: Attributed to Cosmo Alexander, *Portrait of a Jacobite Lady*, mid-eighteenth century, and a portrait of Patrick Grant by Colvin Smith, 1822.

NOTES

INTRODUCTION

1 Donald C. Stewart, *The Setts of the Scottish Tartans* (London: Shepheard-Walwyn Publishers, 1974).
2 Richard Martin, "Transmutations in Tartan: Attributed Meanings to Textile Design," keynote address at the "Symposium of the Textile Society of America," Minneapolis Institute of Art, 1988.
3 Hugh Cheape, *Tartan, The Highland Habit* (Edinburgh: The National Museums of Scotland, 1991), 13.
4 Ibid., 52.
5 Michael Picucci, "Tartan as Ritual in Action," unpublished paper.

TRADITION

1 Richard Martin, *Tartan* (New York: Fashion Institute of Technology, 1988), 1.
2 Hugh Cheape, *Tartan, The Highland Habit* (revised and updated) (Edinburgh: National Museums of Scotland, 2006), 7.
3 Ibid., 11.
4 Hugh Cheape, "Tartan and Scottish Identity," paper delivered at "Decorative Arts at the ROM Symposium," Royal Ontario Museum, 2002.
5 James D. Scarlett, *Tartan, The Highland Textile* (London: Shepheard-Walwyn Publishers, 1990), 46.
6 Hugh Cheape, "Researching Tartan," *Costume: The Journal of the Costume Society* no. 27 (1993): 37.
7 I. F. Grant and Hugh Cheape, *Periods in Highland History* (New York: Barnes & Noble, 2000), 186.
8 R. W. Munro, *Highland Clans and Tartans* (London: Octopus Books, 1977), 14.
9 Martin Martin quoted in Scarlett, *Tartan, The Highland Textile*, 12.
10 John Telfer Dunbar, *History of Highland Dress* (London: Oliver & Boyd, 1962), 2.
11 Cheape, *Tartan, The Highland Habit*, 13.
12 Ira von Furstenburg with Andrew Nicolls, *Tartanware: Souvenirs from Scotland* (London: Pavilion Books Ltd., 1996), 8.
13 Grant and Cheape, 8.
14 Ibid., 126.
15 Cheape, "Researching Tartan," 39.
16 Grant and Cheape, 139.
17 Col. Philip Halford-McLeod, "Tartan Trews," *Military Modelling*, 30.
18 Grant and Cheape, 193.
19 Cheape, *Tartan, The Highland Habit*, 15.
20 Grant and Cheape, 198.
21 Cheape, *Tartan, The Highland Habit*, 31.
22 T. M. Devine, *The Scottish Nation, 1700–2000* (New York: Penguin Books, 2000), 44.
23 Fitzroy Maclean, *Highlander: A History of the Highland Clans* (London: David Campbell Publishers, 1995).
24 Ibid.
25 Dunbar, 3.
26 Cheape, *Tartan, The Highland Habit*, 25.
27 Christian Hesketh, *Tartans* (London: Weidenfeld and Nicolson, 1961), 23.
28 Hugh Cheape, "The Changing Image of the Highlands after 1745," paper delivered at the conference "Benjamin West in Focus," National Galleries of Scotland, 2005.
29 Cheape, *Tartan, The Highland Habit*, 36.
30 Cheape, "The Changing Image of the Highlands after 1745."
31 Donald C. Stewart, *The Setts of the Scottish Tartans* (London: Shepheard-Walwyn Publishers, 1974), 2.
32 As quoted in Malcolm Chapman, *The Celts: The Construction of a Myth* (New York: St. Martin's Press, 1992), 140.
33 Dunbar, 11.
34 Munro, 74.
35 Cheape, *Tartan, The Highland Habit*, 48.
36 Richard Martin, "Transmutations in Tartan: Attributed Meanings to Textile Design," keynote address at the "Symposium of the Textile Society of America," Minneapolis Institute of Art, 1988.
37 Munro, 84.
38 Ibid, 86.
39 Hugh Trevor-Roper, "The Invention of Tradition: The Highland Tradition of Scotland," in *The Invention of Tradition*, eds., Eric Hobsbawm and Terence Ranger (Cambridge: Cambridge University Press, 1983), 30.
40 Both the names "Stewart" and "Stuart" are used for the royal house which ruled the Kingdom of Scotland for over three hundred years (1301-1707), and, briefly, during the reign of Queen Anne. The name "Stewart" derived from the hereditary title of "High Steward." When Mary, Queen of Scots, lived in France, the spelling of the name was changed and "Gallicised" to Stuart, as there is no "w" in French. Both names are in current use, although the Scots prefer to use the original spelling, and when it's used in conjunction with tartan, the name is usually spelled with a "w."
41 Munro, 86.
42 Ibid.
43 Ibid.
44 Trevor-Roper, 30.
45 Robert Clyde, *From Rebel to Hero: The Changing Image of the Highlander, 1745–1830* (Scotland: Tuckwell Press, 1995), 129.
46 John Prebble, *The King's Jaunt* (London: Berlinn Ltd, 2000), 105.

47 Munro, 87.
48 Ann Sutton and Richard Carr, *Tartans, Their Art and History* (New York: Arco Publishing, 1984), 23.
49 Trevor-Roper, 30.
50 Ibid., 31.
51 Munro, 234.
52 Iain Zaczek and Charles Phillips, *The Illustrated Encyclopedia of Tartan* (London: Lorenz Books, 2004), 74.
53 Hesketh, 86.
54 Zaczek and Phillips, 74.

FASHION

1 Cathy Newman, *Fashion* (Washington, D.C.: National Geographic, 2001).
2 Hugh Cheape, *Tartan, The Highland Habit* (Edinburgh: National Museums of Scotland, 1991), 68.
3 Andrew Bolton, *Bravehearts: Men in Skirts* (London: V & A Publishing, 2003), 122.
4 Suzy Menkes, *Windsor Style* (Topsfield: Salem House Publishing, 1988), 6.
5 Ibid., 124.
6 H.R.H. Edward, Duke of Windsor, *Windsor Revisited* (Boston: Houghton, Mifflin, 1960).
7 H.R.H., Edward, Duke of Windsor, *A Family Album* (London: Cassell, 1960), 82.
8 Ibid.
9 Ibid.
10 Frances Lonsdale Donaldson, *Edward VIII* (Philadelphia: Lippincott, 1975), 344.
11 Nicholas Lawford quoted in Wendy Moonan, *New York Times*, February 26, 1998, 1.
12 Rumor has it that the real reason the duke had his pants made in the United States has to do with his sartorial preferences and wartime rationing in England. After World War II, textile use regulations in England prohibited the tailoring of the cuffs the duke insisted on for all of his trousers.
13 Duchess of Windsor, *The Heart Has Its Reasons* (London: Michael Joseph, 1956).
14 H.R.H., Edward, Duke of Windsor, *A Family Album*, 129.
15 Kerry Taylor quoted in Moonan, 1.
16 Colin McDonnell, *Ralph Lauren: The Man, the Vision, the Style* (London: Cassell, 2002), 61.
17 Ibid., 35.
18 Ibid., 59.
19 Newman, 103.
20 Malcolm McLaren, "You Ask the Questions," *The Independent*, January 12, 2000.
21 Peter York, "The Punk Post-Mortem," *Harpers and Queen* (July 1977): 106.
22 Claire Wilcox, *Vivienne Westwood* (London: V&A Publications), 2004.

23 Ibid., 23.
24 Rebecca Arnold, "Vivienne Westwood's Anglomania," in *The Englishness of English Dress*, eds., Christopher Breward, Becky Conekin, and Caroline Cox (Oxford: Berg Publishers, 2002).
25 J. C. Flugel quoted in Newman, 104.
26 Arnold, 161.
27 Ibid., 165.
28 Christopher Breward, *Fashion* (Oxford: Oxford University Press, 2003), 193.
29 Arnold, 168.
30 Ingeborg Harms, "Reaping the Benefit from Dedication," *Vogue* (Germany) (July 2004).
31 Letter to the authors, March 2007.
32 Harms.
33 Wilcox, 26.
34 Isabella Blow, *Harper's Bazaar* (June 1996): 30.
35 Caroline Evans, *Fashion at the Edge* (New Haven: Yale University Press, 2003), 141.
36 Amy Spindler, *New York Times*, March 14, 1995.
37 Miles Socha, "The Real McQueen," *WWD Magazine* (Fall 2006): 9.
38 William Gibson, "A Most Benevolent Marvel," in *You Can Find Inspiration in Everything (And if You Can't, Look Again)* by Paul Smith (London: Violette Eds., 2001), 74–85.
39 Suzy Menkes, *International Herald Tribune*, April 18, 1989, 7.

LIVING

1 Joan Kron, *Home-Psych: The Social Psychology of Home and Decoration* (New York: Clarkson Potter, 1983), xviii.
2 Ted Loos, "Scotch Neat," *Elle Décor* no. 89 (February/March 2002): 126.
3 Ibid., 132.
4 Elaine Louie, "Lauren, Forever Plaid," *New York Times*, April 11, 1991.
5 Gregory Cerio, "Honey, I'm Home," *House and Garden* (April, 2001): 178.
6 Joan Kron, "Welcome to the Fun House," *Home Style* (December 2001/January 2002): 50.
7 William Diamond and Anthony Baratta, *Diamond Baratta Design* (New York: Bulfinch Press, 2006), 7.
8 Cerio, 178.
9 Diamond and Baratta, 7.
10 Elspeth Thompson, "Tartan Traveler," *The World of Interiors* (October 1993): 151.
11 Interview with the authors, February 2007.
12 M. J. Madigan, Visual Store.com, July 22, 2003.
13 Iain Zaczek, *World Tartans* (New York: Barnes & Noble, 2001), 13.

BIBLIOGRAPHY

Arnold, Rebecca. "Vivienne Westwood's Anglomania." In *The Englishness of English Dress*. Edited by Christopher Breward, Becky Conekin, and Caroline Cox. Oxford: Berg, 2002.

Bain, Robert. *Clans and Tartans of Scotland*. Expanded and edited by Margaret O. MacDougall. London and Glasgow: Wm. Collins & Sons, Ltd., 1968.

Barber, E.J.W. *Prehistoric Textiles: The Development of Cloth in the Neolithic and Bronze Age*. Princeton: Princeton University Press, 1991.

Bolton, Andrew. *Bravehearts: Men in Skirts*. London: V&A Publishing, 2003.

Breward, Christopher. *Fashion*. Oxford: Oxford University Press, 2003.

Chapman, Malcolm. *The Celts: The Construction of a Myth*. New York: St. Martin's Press, 1992.

Cheape, Hugh. "The Changing Image of the Highlands after 1745." Paper delivered at the conference "Benjamin West in Focus," National Galleries of Scotland, 2005.

————. "Researching Tartan." *Costume: The Journal of the Costume Society* no. 27 (1993).

————. "Tartan and Scottish Identity." Paper delivered at "Decorative Arts at the ROM Symposium," Royal Ontario Museum, 2002.

————. *Tartan, The Highland Habit*. Edinburgh: National Museums of Scotland. 1991.

Clyde, Robert. *From Rebel to Hero: The Changing Image of the Highlander 1745–1830*. Scotland: Tuckwell Press, 1995.

Colgrave, Stephen, and Christopher Sullivan. *Punk, The Definitive Record of a Revolution*. London: Cassell & Co., 2001.

Collie, George P. *Highland Dress*. London: Penguin Books, 1948.

Devine, T. M. *The Scottish Nation, 1700–2000*. New York: Penguin Books, 2000.

Diamond, William, Anthony Baratta, and Dan Shaw. *Diamond Baratta Design*. New York and Boston: Bulfinch Press, 2006.

The Duke and Duchess of Windsor: The Private Collections. New York: Sotheby's, 1997.

Dunbar, John Telfer. *Highland Costume*. London: Oliver & Boyd, 1977.

————. *History of Highland Dress*. London: Oliver & Boyd, 1962.

Eicher, Joanne B. *Dress & Ethnicity: Change Across Space and Time*. Oxford: Berg, 1995.

Evans, Caroline. *Fashion at the Edge*. New Haven: Yale University Press, 2003.

Grant, I. F., and Hugh Cheape. *Periods in Highland History*. New York: Barnes & Noble, 2000.

Harms, Ingeborg. "Reaping the Benefit from Dedication." *Vogue* (Germany) (July 2004).

Hesketh, Christian. *Tartans*. London: Weidenfeld and Nicolson, 1961.

H.R.H. Edward, Duke of Windsor. *A Family Album*. London: Cassell, 1960.

————. *The King's Story*. New York: G.P. Putnam's Sons, 1947.

Kinross, Lord. *The Windsor Years: The Life of Edward, as Prince of Wales, King, and Duke of Windsor*. Middlesex: Penguin Books, 1967.

Koda, Harold, Richard Martin, and Laura Sinderbrand. *Tartan*. Exhibition catalogue. New York: Fashion Institute of Technology, 1988.

Kron, Joan. *Home Psych: The Social Psychology of Home and Decoration*. New York: Clarkson Potter, 1983.

Lehu, Jean-Marc. *Brand Rejuvenation*. London: Rogan. 2006.

Loos, Ted. "Scotch Neat." *Elle Décor* (February/March 2002).

Mackie, J. D. *A History of Scotland*. London: Penguin, 1964.

MacLean, Fitzroy. *Highlander: A History of the Highland Clans*. London: David Campbell, 1995.

————. *Scotland: A Concise History*. London: Thames and Hudson, 1970.

Martin, Richard. "Transmutations in Tartan: Attributed Meanings to Textile Design." Keynote address at the Symposium of the Textile Society of America, Minneapolis Institute of Art, 1988.

McDonnell, Colin. *Ralph Lauren: The Man, the Vision, the Style*. London: Cassell, 2002.

Menkes, Suzy. *Windsor Style*. Topsfield: Salem House Publishing, 1988.

Munro, R. W. *Highland Clans and Tartan*. London: Octopus Publishers, 1977.

Newman, Cathy. *Fashion*. Washington, D.C.: National Geographic, 2001.

Prebble, John. *The Highland Clearances*. London: Martin, Secker & Warburg, Ltd., 1963; second edition published by Penguin Books, 1969.

Smith, Paul. *You Can Find Inspiration in Everything (And if You Can't, Look Again)*. London: Violette Eds, 2001.

Stewart, Donald C. *The Setts of the Scottish Tartans*. London: Shepheard-Walwyn Publishers, 1974.

Sutton, Ann, and Richard Carr. *Tartans, Their Art and History*. New York: Arco Publishing, 1984.

Taylor, Lou. *The Study of Dress History*. Manchester and New York: Manchester University Press, 2002.

Thompson, Elspeth. "Tartan Traveler." *World of Interiors* (October 1993).

Trevor-Roper, Hugh, "The Invention of Tradition: The Highland Tradition of Scotland." In *The Invention of Tradition*. Edited by Eric Hobsbawm and Terence Ranger. Cambridge: Cambridge University Press, 1983.

Von Furstenberg, Ira with Andrew Nicolls. *Tartanware: Souvenirs from Scotland*. London: Pavilion Books Ltd., 1990.

Wilcox, Claire. *Vivienne Westwood*. London: V&A Publications, 2004.

York, Peter. "The Punk Post-Mortem." *Harpers & Queen* (July 1977).

Zaczek, Iain. *World Tartans*. New York: New York: Barnes & Noble. 2001.

Zaczek, Iain, and Charles Phillips. *The Illustrated Encyclopedia of Tartan*. London: Lorenz Books, 2004.

From left to right: A sporran bag against a rich red dress by Gianni Penati, *Vogue*/© Condé Nast Publications/CORBIS; a classic Burberry bag from the Icons collection, 2007; Vivienne Westwood boots for 9 West; and a detail of a kilt.

SHOPPING FOR TARTAN

Wherein we present the best kilt and tartan purveyors worldwide, as well as a list of designers who feature tartan in their fashion and home accessories lines or use it in their interior design work.

KILTS AND HIGHLAND DRESS AND ACCESSORIES

HOUSE OF EDGAR
Tower House, Ruthvenfield Road
Inveralmond Perth, Scotland, UK PH1 3UN
Tel: 44 1738 604051   Fax: 44 1738 604010

The House of Edgar stocks over eight hundred clan, district, and Irish county tartans in a variety of weights and compositions, as well as a wide selection of Highland dress items including jackets, sporrans, ties, and brogues. They also stock giftware and tableware.

INGLES BUCHAN
Mercat Building, 26 Gallowgate
Glasgow, Scotland, UK G1 5AB
Tel: 44 141 553 1530   Fax: 44 141 553 1527
info@inglesbuchan.com

Ingles Buchan is a family firm that manufactures over five hundred authentic Scottish tartans using 100 percent pure new wool woven in Scotland and sixty other products, including ties, scarves, bow ties, sashes, and much more.

JAMES JOHNSTON & COMPANY OF ELGIN LIMITED
Johnstons Newmill
Elgin
Morayshire, Scotland, UK IV30 4AF
Tel: 44 1343 554040
info@JohnstonsCashmere.com
www.johnstonscashmere.com

Johnstons has been manufacturing cashmere and fine woollens incorporating many tartans since 1797 and is renowned worldwide as the pioneer of Estate Tweed. Alongside their own label they remain the "name behind the names" and supply many leading couture houses and fashion independents including Hermès, Louis Vuitton, Chanel, among others. The original mill is in the Highlands and their factory in the Scottish Borders, but they have showrooms in London, Germany, New York, and Japan.

LOCHCARRON
Waverley Mill, Rodgers Road
Selkirk, Scotland, UK TD7 5DX
Tel: 44 1750 726000   Fax: 44 1750 724100
quality@lochcarron.com

In the US
Tel: 603 356 3369   Fax: 603 356 2554
info@lochcarronusa.com

In Canada
Tel: 705 728 4932   Fax: 705 728 5923
info@lochcarroncanada.com

Worldwide Retail Outlets
Burnett's and Struth (Canada)
Designs on Cashmere (Scotland)

CoolKilts.com
McKenzies (England)
Scottish Lion (US)

Lochcarron offers the world's largest range of authentic tartans, Highland dress, and accessories (including sporrans, belts, shoes, socks, ties, and scarves) for body and home. They also create kilts made-to-measure.

MY OWN TARTAN
www.myowntartan.com

A wonderful new company created in Scotland which will allow you to work with its design team not only to create your own tartan, but also to weave the fabric and make the final garment.

STRATHMORE WOOLLEN COMPANY LIMITED
Station Works, North Street
Forfar, Angus Scotland, UK DD8 3BN
Tel: 44 1307 462135   Fax: 44 1307 468603
www.tartanbystrathmore.co.uk

Strathmore Woollen Company supplies authentic tartan throughout the world as well as a range of other related products. A stock service is now offered to customers in over five hundred designs in two high-quality worsted kilting and skirting fabrics.

SWAINE ADENEY BRIGG
54 St. James's Street, London, UK SW1A
Tel: 44 20 7409 7277

In the US:
Sterling & Burke Ltd
1025 Connecticut Avenue NW, Suite 1012
Washington, DC 20036
Tel: 800 205 7739 or 202 331 4244
SwaineAdeneyBrigg@SterlingAndBurke.com

Swaine Adeney was founded in 1750 in Piccadilly, conveniently near the Royal Mews, and made exclusive travel goods and business cases. They received their first Royal Warrant from King George III for carriage driving whips and have received Royal Warrants from each successive monarch thereafter. In 1943 they joined together with Brigg and Son, the royal umbrella makers, established in 1836 at St. James's Street, London. An exclusive mix of exquisite materials and rarefied expertise, the Swaine Adeney Brigg umbrella has become an international byword for the very best of British craftsmanship.

21st CENTURY KILTS
Tel: 44 131 226 1555
enquiries@geoffreykilts.co.uk
www.21stcenturykilts.com

Innovative young designer Howie Nicholsby has updated traditional kilt design. Using fabrications not usually associated with kilts, like banker's pin stripes, camouflage fabrics, and denim, Nicholsby has created a business that has been embraced by young people of all ages around the world. He also designs kilt suits that replace the usual trouser with a kilt bottom and a tailored jacket in matching fabrics. His designs have a devoted celebrity following including Scottish musician KT Tunstall and actors Vin Diesel, Robbie Williams, and Alan Cumming.

DESIGNERS WHO LOVE TARTAN

ABERCROMBIE & FITCH
720 Fifth Avenue
New York, NY 10019
Tel: 212 381 0110

Founded in 1892, the company was for many decades an elite excursion goods retailer. In 1988 the company was repositioned as a lifestyle brand catering to a young, college-age audience. They offer a wide range of plaid and tartan clothing items.

ANTA SCOTLAND LTD
Fearn
Tàin
Inverness
Highland, Scotland, UK IV20 1XW
Tel: 44 1862 832477   Fax: 44 1862 832616
sales@anta.co.uk
www.anta.co.uk

Crocket's Land
91–93 West Bow
Victoria Street
Edinburgh, Scotland, UK EH1 2JP
Tel./Fax: 44 131 225 4616
Anta-edinburgh@btconnect.com
55 Sloan Square
London, UK SW1W 8AX
Tel: 44 20 77304773   Fax: 44 20 77304789

ANTA specializes in fabrics and ceramics and has contemporary versions of traditional designs such as tartans. They will custom design and color tartan fabrics to your specifications for both home and clothing.

BROOKS BROTHERS
US Stores
346 Madison Ave
New York, NY 10017
Tel: 212 682 8800
www.brooksbrothers.com

666 Fifth Avenue
New York, NY 10103
Tel: 212 261 9440

UK Stores
Old Bond Street
London EC2N 1DW
Tel: 44 207 256 6013

132–34 Regent Street
London W1B 5SJ
Tel: 44 20 3 238 0030

In 1818 Henry Sands Brooks founded Brooks Brothers, the first ready-to-wear fashion emporium in America. Tartan plaid is a perennial at Brooks Brothers, from boy's pajamas to duffel coats to boxers and their classic broadcloth button-down shirts.

BURBERRY
21–23 New Bond Steet
London, UK WIS 2RE
Tel: 44 20 7968 0000
www.burberry.com

9 East 57th Street
New York, NY 10022
Tel: 212 407 7100

Burberry is one of the best internationally recognized luxury brands in the world, known for its signature tartan (or check) as well as its quality rainwear and fashion. Burberry's offerings extend to clothing for the whole family including infants as well as items for the home.

CHRISTIAN LACROIX
73, rue du Faubourg-Saint-Honoré
Paris, France 75008
Tel: 33 1 42 68 79 04
www.christian-lacroix.fr

2–4, place Saint-Sulpice
Paris, France 75006
Tel: 33 1 46 33 48 95

366, rue Saint-Honoré
Paris, France 75001
Tel: 33 1 42 61 39 08

Couturier Christian Lacroix is known for his whimsically beautiful couture and ready-to-wear creations. His extravagant use of textiles range from classic tartan plaids to over-blown floral silks, often in the sunny colors of his native Provence.

GREAT SCOT—IMPORTERS OF FINE SCOTTISH GOODS
P.O. Box 1817
Nashville, Indiana 47448
Tel: 800 572 1073
greatscot@hughes.net
www.greatscotshop.com

A great source for clan crest items, tartan scarves, ties, Celtic jewelry, and just about anything to do with Scotland and the Highlands. Everything from tartan fabric yardage to needlepoint Celtic emblems is available here. Kilt rentals are also available.

ISAAC MIZRAHI
www.isaacmizrahiny.com

Isaac Mizrahi and his brilliant designs using bold colors and pattern (including tartan plaid) are available in several different lines. For Isaac Mizrahi New York see his online store at www.isaacmizrahiny.com, for his couture and demi-couture go to Bergdorf Goodman in New York City, and for his popular, very accessibly priced collection Isaac Mizrahi for Target, go to www.target.com.

JEAN-PAUL GAULTIER
France Stores
44, Avenue George V
Paris 75008
Tel: 33 1 44 43 00 44   Fax: 33 1 44 43 00 45
www.jeanpaulgaultier.com

French designer Jean-Paul Gaultier who designs his own couture and ready-to-wear as well as Hermès's sportswear, is renowned for dressing Madonna and advocating skirts for men. He is a great devotee of tartan plaid and has used it extensively throughout his various collections.

MARC JACOBS
Collection Ready-to-Wear, Accessories, Shoes, Men's
163 Mercer Street
New York, NY 10012
Tel: 212 343 1490   Fax: 212 343 2423
www.marcjacobs.com

Collection Accessories, Shoes
385 Bleecker Street
New York, NY 10014
Tel: 212 924 6126   Fax: 212 924 6504

Marc By Marc Jacobs Ready-to-Wear, Accessories, Shoes, Men's
403–05 Bleecker Street
New York, NY 10014
Tel: 212 924 0026

One of the most celebrated designers currently working, Marc Jacobs has the innate ability to fathom what we want before we know. He has featured tartan in his highly coveted collections for Louis Vuitton, which has many stores throughout the world. To find which stores carry ready-to-wear and accessories please visit www.louisvuitton.com.

MICHAEL KAYE COUTURE
270 West 39th Street
New York, NY 10018
Tel: 917 295 1555
mkcouture@mac.com

A dyed-in-the-wool fan of tartan, the Canadian-born Kaye, uses the fabric in many of his collections of custom-designed women's clothing—including a tartan gown that resides in the permanent collection of the Costume Institute of The Metropolitan Museum of Art in New York.

OLD ENGLAND
12, boulevard des Capucines
Paris, France 75009
Tel: 33 1 47 42 81 99
www.old-england.fr

Old England was founded in 1867 in response to the enthusiastic reception the French gave to British style and quality after the two countries had signed a free-trade agreement. In addition to their world-famous duffel coats, a discerning clientele can find twin knits in fine cashmere, traditional tartan wrap skirts, Scottish tartan mufflers, tailor-made men's shirts and suits, quality shoes, and many stylish accessories.

PAUL SMITH
Westbourne House
122 Kensington Park Road
London, UK W11 2EP
Tel: 44 20 7727 3553
www.paulsmith.co.uk.

40/44 Floral Street
London, UK WC2E 9DG
Tel: 44 20 7379 7133

The Courtyard Royal Exchange
London, UK EC3 3LQ
Tel: 44 20 7626 4778

US Stores
142 Greene Street
New York, NY 10012
Tel: 646 613 3060

(Men only)
108 Fifth Avenue
New York, NY 10011
Tel: 212 627 9770

Within twenty years of his introduction to fashion, Sir Paul Smith (knighted by H.M. Queen Elizabeth II) has established himself as the preeminent British designer. He manages to transmit a genuine sense of humor and mischief mixed with his love of tradition and the classics, including tartan.

RALPH LAUREN
867 Madison Avenue
New York, NY 10021
Tel: 212 606 2100
For a list of Ralph Lauren's stores worldwide please visit www.polo.com.

Boys' Store
878 Madison Avenue
New York, NY 10021
Tel: 212 606 3376

379 West Broadway
New York, NY 10012
Tel: 212 625 1660

R. SCOTT FRENCH
485 Seventh Ave, Suite 908
New York, NY 10018
Tel: 212 760 0078
scott@rscottfrench.com
www.rscottfrench.com

R. Scott French is a contemporary designer collection of both men's and women's sportswear that incorporates tartan frequently.

STUBBS AND WOOTTON
1034 Lexington Ave
New York, NY 10021
Tel: 212 249 5200
www.stubbsandwootton.com

14 Jobs Lane
Southampton, NY 11968
Tel: 631 283 7332

4 Via Parigi
Palm Beach, FL 33411
Tel: 561 655 6857

The Stubbs and Wootton legacy: a tradition of designing and handcrafting in Europe unique shoes and slippers for ladies and gentlemen. If it's tartan slippers you are desirous of, Stubbs and Wootton can custom make them for you in needlepoint or fabric, with or without your initials.

TIFFANY & CO.
727 Fifth Avenue
New York, NY 10022
Tel: 212 755 8000
www.tiffany.com

UK Store
25 Old Bond Street
London W1S 4QB
Tel: 44 207 409 2790

Since 1837, Tiffany & Co. has established itself worldwide as the pinnacle of good taste and matchless service. From jewelry to china, from fine crystal to watches, from stationary to bridal gifts, Tiffany has it all. In addition they have a wonderful corporate gift service which supplies custom trophies and recognition gifts. Be sure to check out their holiday plaid chinaware. There are many Tiffany Outlets throughout the United States, Europe, and Asia.

VIVIENNE WESTWOOD LTD.
Westwood Studios
9–15 Elcho Street,
London, UK SW11 4AU
Tel: 44 20 7924 4747   Fax: 44 20 7738 9655
info@viviennewestwood.co.uk
www.viviennewestwoodonline.co.uk

Fashion's leading maverick since the '70s, the highly acclaimed Dame Vivienne Westwood has continually used tartan—often outrageously—in her various collections. She has been honored by solo shows at the Victoria and Albert Museum in London and around the world. The Westwood empire ranges from day and evening clothes for women and men to accessories.

INTERIOR DESIGNERS

DIAMOND AND BARATTA
270 Lafayette Street
New York, NY 10012
Tel: 212 966 8892
www.DiamondBarattaDesign.com

Bold, colorful, and ultra-creative are just three words that come to mind when one thinks of the incomparable work, both traditional and contemporary, of designers William Diamond and Anthony Baratta, who have designed extraordinary homes all over the country.

RANDALL A. RIDLESS
315 West 39th Street, Suite 1104
New York, NY 10018
Tel: 212 643 8140   Fax: 212 643 8155
Info@RandallRidless.com

Randall A. Ridless is a New York–based interior designer who founded his eponymous interior design consulting firm in 1999. Ridless created the Burberry prototype store on Bond Street in London. His worldwide designs for Burberry now include stores in Tokyo, Barcelona, Moscow, New York City, Chicago, Beverly Hills, San Francisco, among many others. Ridless' current residential projects include homes in Manhattan, Palm Beach, and Bridgehampton, and he has recently been signed on to renovate Fifth Avenue's landmark Lord & Taylor.

Right: Ronald Cheape, son of tartan scholar Hugh Cheape, in the uniform of the Pipe Major, Pipes, and Drums of the Edinburgh Academy, 2003.

ACKNOWLEDGMENTS

The authors would like to acknowledge the talent, commitment, and efforts of those people who helped shepherd this book into being:

Hugh Cheape, principal curator at the National Museums of Scotland—our bottomless thanks for sharing your time, research, hospitality, and extraordinary erudition with us, both in Edinburgh and in e-mail; we will forever be in your debt.

Rizzoli International, our publishers: David Morton, our "godfather" whose sage counsel helped steer us in the right direction; and Isabel Venero, our stalwart editor, who was tireless in the trenches. In addition, Helen Pratt, our agent, whose enthusiasm for the subject and belief in us was unflagging.

Rose Marie Bravo, vice-chairman Burberry Group plc and former CEO of Burberry, who was one of the first to share our enthusiasm about the possibility of a tome on plaid and whose foreword adds a grace-note to our book.

Our art director, Paul McKevitt, whose prior experience with tartan was limited to a fondness for The Bay City Rollers.

Karen Broderick, our photo researcher whose gentle but unrelenting pursuit of hard-to-find images is unmatched. Eric Rachlis of Getty Images whose early support of our project was key. Condé Nast's Leigh Montville, Shawn Waldron (and Fairchild's) Molly Monosky for their patience and willingness to help.

We are forever grateful to the designers whose tartan talent brims from our pages:

Ralph Lauren; Marc Jacobs; Christopher Bailey; Paul Smith; Isaac Mizrahi; Michael Kaye; Robert Rufino; Bill Diamond and Tony Baratta; Ward Denton and Christopher Gardner; Randall A. Ridless; Annie Stewart of ANTA; and R. Scott French—all of whom took the time to talk tartan with us at length. Vivienne Westwood and Alexander McQueen who supplied us with information and materials. Photographer Bruce Weber for his compelling Abercrombie & Fitch images; artist Mark Beard whose towering tartan paintings are a story in themselves; and Geoffrey Carroll, mastermind of "Dressed to Kilt."

Dress historians Valerie Steele, chief curator of the Museum at F.I.T.; Harold Koda, curator in charge of the Costume Institute at the Metropolitan Museum of Art; and Joanne Eicher, regents professor, University of Minnesota, for imparting their expertise on tartan. Thanks also to architect Jaquelin T. Robertson for his beautifully penned quotes.

Our appreciation, too, to those who helped provide the designer photographs, materials, and support: especially, Erika Johnston, Pat Doherty, and Elsie Voloel at Burberry; Patricia Christman and Melissa Pathay at Ralph Lauren; Brigitte Stepputtis at Vivienne Westwood; Jenny Lurie at Isaac Mizrahi; Emma Stirling and Colette Youell at Paul Smith; Kate Waters at Marc Jacobs; Connie Uzzo, formerly of Yves St. Laurent; Elizabeth Machin for ANTA; Samantha Gore at Randall A. Ridless; Linda Buckley, Tiffany's vice-president of media relations; Nathan Kilcher at Little Bear, Inc.; Aiden Aldred at Alexander McQueen; Kerry Youmans at KCD; and Irving Solero at F.I.T.

Niall McInerney for his generosity with both time and photographs; Thom Gilbert for his gorgeous photographs; Stephanie Goldman for her gracious hospitality; and architect Enda Donaher for his flawless drawings.

Thanks to John Haffner Layden for his editorial guidance and precision; Lewis Esson for his support and historical expertise; Michael Picucci for his take on tartan-psych; David Winkler for his lyrical "Tartanscape"; and Ki Hackney for sharing her wisdom, experience, and counsel.

In addition, Jeffrey would like to express his personal gratitude to: Stan Herman for his undying friendship and unconditional support; Jason Hardison for his wonderful photographs and constant caring; Peggy Tagliarino for her constant nagging; Pamela Clarke Keogh, Michael Schwarz, Teri Agins, and Louis Falcone; and last, but not least, Eleanor Banks for always being there, no matter what.

Doria would like to extend her personal thanks to: my husband, Philippe, and sons, Christian and Justin, for tolerating both "the tartan war room" and endless take-out; Margaret Knowlton for her always interesting clippings; Anya Robertson, Marcia Schaeffer, and my entire tennis network for their friendship and support; Bob Ingersole for the patience of Job; Bernadette Kathryn and Donn Nelson for their soothing care; and everlasting thanks to my late parents, Julia and Louis Martinelli, who must have saved every word I ever wrote.

MODEL AND PHOTO CREDITS

LINDA EVANGELISTA, represented by dna Model Management, New York: 30-31, 46, 125, 141, 144, 181, 183, 185, 198-99

KATE MOSS, represented by Storm Models, London: 33, 140, 152-53, 156-57

STELLA TENNANT, represented by dna Model Management, New York: 148

JOHN BALSOM: 149

GILLES BENSIMON: 132

LLOYD BISHOP FOR "DRESSED TO KILT": 260, 265

CHRISTINE A. BUTLER: 280-81

BLAIR CASTLE, PERTHSHIRE: 64

BRIDGEMAN ART LIBRARY: 54, National Trust of Scotland/Fyvie Castle Collection, Scotland; 60, © National Museum of Scotland; 70, private collection, © Philip Mould Historical Portraits, Ltd., London, UK; 76, 283, The Drambuie Collection, Edinburgh, Scotland; 80-81, The British Library, London, UK © British Library Board; 62, all rights reserved; 93, Roy Miles Fine Paintings; 106, © Forbes Magazine Collection, NY

BURBERRY: 248, 249, 287

CATWALKING.COM: 33

© ROBERT CECATO: 150-51, 155 (upper left, upper right, and lower right)

© JAMES COCHRANE: 158

PATRICK DEMARCHELIER: 199

FRANCOIS DISCHINGER: 236-37

EVERETT COLLECTION, © HBO: 273

FIRST VIEW: Marcio Madeira for First View, 164, 166, 167, 175, 201, 204, 205

FORBES ARCHIVES: 279

RALPH LAUREN HOME COLLECTION: 223 (top)

LENDON FLANAGAN: 234

TIM GEANEY: 126

GETTY IMAGES: 8, Tim Graham; 10, Frank Micelotta /© Getty Images; 13, Fox Photos; 14-5, Chaloner Woods; 16, Hulton Archive; 17: Hulton Archive/© Getty Images; 18, Hulton Archive/© Getty Images; 19, Hulton Archive/Getty Images; 22-23, Hulton Archive; 25, Evening Standard; 27, Time Life Pictures Inc./ Pictures Inc.; 38, Chaloner Woods/Hulton Archive; 40, Silver Screen Collection/Hulton Archive; 41,

Otto Dyar/Hulton Archive: 42-43, John Kobal Foundation; 49, Frank Micelotta/Fox via Getty Images; 50, Robert John/Fotos International; 52, Dave Hogan/Hulton Archive; 72, 88-89, 101, 105, Hulton Archive; 108, second from left, John Brown/Express/Express; 112, lower right, Fox Photos; 121; 135, Robin Platzer/Twin Images; 136, Jeff J. Mitchell; 171, M.J. Kim; 188-89, Ian Showell/Keystone/Hulton Archive/© 2005 Getty Images; 209, Central Press/© Getty Images; 252-53, Santi Visalli, Inc.; 256, Central Press; 257, Topical Press; 258, Evening Standard; 259, Frank Micelotte/© Getty Images; 261, MGM Studios/Courtesy Getty Images; 264, Giulio Marcocchi/© 2003 Getty Images; 266, William Philpott; 267, Nick Wilson/Allsport; 268, Ryan McVay for Photodisc Red; 270-71, Reg Lancaster/Express; 274-75, Fox Photos; 276, upper left, Christopher Furlong; 276, upper right, Getty Images; 276, lower left, Jeff J. Mitchell/© 2006 Getty Images; 276, lower right, Tim Graham Picture Library; 277, Ken Goff/Time Life Pictures; 278, Terry Smith/Time Life Pictures/© Terry Smith; 287, Getty Images; 288, Tom Raymond

THOM GILBERT: 160 (right), 200-1, 245

OBERTO GILI: 47, 129, 131 (lower left), 132 (left and right)

TRIA GIOVAN: 206, 226

FRANCOIS HALARD for RALPH LAUREN: 225

THIBAULT JEANSON: 45, 208, 210, 211, 212, 214, 215, 216-17, 218, 219

MICHAEL KAYE: 272

THOMAS KELLER: 162, 186, 187

© KEYSTONE: 112 (lower left), The Illustrated London New Picture Library

KOBAL COLLECTION: 262, Talisman, United Artists/The Kobal Collection/James David; 263, Icon/ Ladd Co. Paramount

RICHARD LEAROYD: 90, from a private collection

DAN LECCA: 179, 182, 183

RAY MAIN: 1, 242, 243

MARY EVANS PICTURE LIBRARY: 21, 29, 102-3, 108-9 (third from right)

NIALL MCINERNEY: 3, 32, 110, 134, 137, 139, 140, 141, 142, 143, 144, 145, 147

JAMES MERRELL: 230, 231, 233

MIRRORPIX: 20

NATIONAL GALLERIES OF SCOTLAND: 79 (upper left), courtesy NMS; 79 (upper right), © National Galleries of Scotland

NATIONAL GALLERY OF ART, WASHINGTON, D.C.: Collection of Mr. and Mrs. Paul Mellon. © 2006 Board of Trustees, National Gallery of Art

NATIONAL MUSEUMS OF SCOTLAND: 56; 67; 73; 77; 79, National Galleries of Scotland; 82; 86, Scottish National Portrait Gallery; 97, 104

PAUL SMITH: 170, 172, 173

RICHARD PHIBBS: 131

PHOTO 12.COM/Jean Marie Perier: 202-3

RETNA: 28, Patrick Lichfield/Camera Press; 51, photo by Peter Mazel/Sunshine; 112, Bertram Park/Camera Press; 114, photo by Ken Adlard/Camera Press; 117, Patrick Lichfield/Camera Press; 118-19, Patrick Lichfield/Camera Press; 122-23, Ken Adlard/Camera Press

ROTARY: 112

ROYAL COLLECTION, © 2006 H.M. Queen Elizabeth II: 78, 85, 98 (photo by Antonia Reeves)

MARTIN RUSSOCKI, property of WREC: 250, 251

SCOTTISH NATIONAL PORTRAIT GALLERY, © National Galleries of Scotland: 12, 65, 68, 70, 283

DAVID SEIDNER ARCHIVE, © International Center of Photography: 35

IRVING SOLERO: 133 (for F.I.T. Tartan exhibit; Suit lent to The Museum Courtesy of Mohamed Al-Fayed, Chairman of Harrods and Custodian of the Windsor Residence), courtesy the Museum at F.I.T.

SOTHEBY'S PICTURE LIBRARY, LONDON: 99

JENNIFER STEIFLE: 246

LACHLAN STEWART: 239 (lower left and lower right)

MARTHA SWOPE: 254-55

V. SZAREJKO: 227, 228, 229

© MARIO TESTINO: 148, 152-53, 156-57

JOHN TILBERI: 53

TOPHAM: 115, © Topham/The Image Works

FRITZ VON DER SCHULENBERGER, © World of Interiors: 240-41

V&A IMAGES, ALL RIGHTS RESERVED: 108 (first and fourth)

BRUCE WEBER: Bruce Weber for Abercrombie & Fitch: 18, 44; for Ralph Lauren: 124, 127, 128, 130, 131 (upper right and lower right), 133; for Jeffrey Banks: 196, 197

SIMON WHEELER: 238, 239 (upper left and upper right)

RICHARD YOUNG: 174

First published in the United States in 2007 by

Rizzoli International Publications, Inc.
300 Park Avenue South
New York, NY 10010
www.rizzoliusa.com

Copyright © 2007 Jeffrey Banks and Doria de La Chapelle
Foreword copyright © 2007 Rose Marie Bravo

*All efforts have been made to identify copyright holders of images. If a credit is incorrect, please contact the publisher.

2007 2008 2009 2010 / 10 9 8 7 6 5 4 3 2 1

ISBN 10: 0-8478-2982-0
ISBN 13: 978-0-8478-2982-8

Library of Congress Control Number: 2007926136